Get Out of Your Own Way

Uncover the
Source of Happiness
in Golf and Life

By Sam Jarman

Copyright Sam Jarman

First Published April 2023 by Sam Jarman
Print Edition

This book remains the copyrighted property of the author and may not be redistributed to others for commercial or non-commercial purposes.

If you enjoyed this book, please encourage your friends to purchase a copy from their favourite retailer. It is also available in eBook and audiobook formats.

Thank you for your support.

A catalogue record for this book is available from the British Library

Print ISBN: 978-0-9935734-9-1

Cover image by taka1022, distributed under license by Shutterstock.com

Any information offered in this book should not be treated as a substitute for professional medical advice.

Any use of the information in this book is at the reader's discretion and risk. The author cannot be held responsible for any loss, claim or damage arising out of the use, or misuse of the information in this book, or for any material on third party websites.

Table of Contents

Acknowledgements   v
Epigraph   ix

Part One: A Different Understanding   1
Chapter 1: Introduction   3
Chapter 2: Learn Something   15
Chapter 3: The Problem of Belief   29
Chapter 4: Mind Over Golf   43
Chapter 5: The One, Single Cause of Pressure   57
Chapter 6: Who Are You?   73
Summing Up Part One: A New Understanding   93

Part Two: Implications   99
Chapter 7: The Truth About Confidence   101
Chapter 8: The Source of Creativity   115
Chapter 9: The Most Consistent Thing You Know   131
Chapter 10: Understanding Concentration   145
Chapter 11: Maintaining Composure   161
Summing Up Part Two: The Implications   175

Part Three: What Does Golf Mean to You?   181
Chapter 12: The Search for Meaning   183
Chapter 13: A Psychological Theory of Meaning   199
Chapter 14: An Alternative to Psychology   215

Chapter 15: Did You Choose to Play Golf?	229
Chapter 16: Conclusion	245
Bibliography	259
Author's note	261
About the Author	263

Acknowledgements

As I noted in the forward to *The Three Principles of Outstanding Golf*, I didn't set out to write a book. So with hindsight, the fact there are now three of them is a bit of a surprise.

My understanding moved on almost the moment the first book was published. I knew there were things in *Three Principles* that needed clarification. As I was writing *Take Relief*, it quickly became clear that there was a big gap from where I had left things, to where I was then. So, TR became a bridge across that gap. *Get Out of Your Own Way* will hopefully move the reader on once again. Taken as a series, they describe the path I have followed so far.

The understanding that underpins these ideas is not new. It has been around for thousands of years. It is sometimes referred to as the perennial philosophy, as it seems to resurface in one form or another in every age and civilisation. It is the foundation of all the mainstream religions and spiritual traditions. All I have tried to do is express it in a way that I hope is relevant and helpful for a golfer who is frustrated with their current approach to the game.

There are many people I would like to thank for their inspiration, help and support along the way. Over the past 40 years or so, writers and teachers such as Jean Klein, Alan Watts, Francis Lucille, Rupert Spira and others, have given us the language and grammar to speak about these matters in societies and cultures where they have been long overlooked. My own understanding has been deepened by reading and listening to them all.

My thinking, writing, and coaching has been strongly influenced by the works of Dr Bernardo Kastrup, and Nassim Nicholas Taleb. Both are prolific writers and speakers and I recommend following both if the ideas in this book resonate with you.

My friends and fellow coaches Karl Morris, Danny Newcombe, Rich Hudson, Jason Rance and Richard Cheetham have all contributed key ideas through the conversations we have had over recent months. Their curiosity and questions have helped to clarify my thinking and refine my writing.

It has been a pleasure to work with editor Joel Drazner once again. His patience, depth of understanding, attention to detail and incisive questioning helped keep me on track and away from interesting but irrelevant diversions.

Julia Jarman, who remains in her seventies a far better and more prolific author than I will ever be.

Her love of books and the written word was a constant theme throughout my childhood and was clearly more of an inspiration than I realised at the time.

Phil Hughes, Ian Jennions, Malcolm Lewis, Simon Mundie, Martin Wells and numerous others who offered comments, feedback, and encouragement during the writing process.

Mike Wood at Aprilsky.biz for his help and advice with the cover design.

Lastly, my friends, coaching clients and fellow golfers at Woburn and elsewhere, for your friendship, feedback, support and companionship on and off the golf course. Hopefully the continuing conversation has made the game a more enjoyable experience for us all.

Get Out of Your Own Way
Uncover the Source of Happiness in Golf and Life

'You are not your job.
You are not how much money you have in the bank.
You are not the car you drive.
You are not the content of your wallet.
*You are not your ******* khakis.'*

Tyler Durden, from the book Fight Club,
by Chuck Palahniuk

PART ONE

A Different Understanding

CHAPTER 1

Introduction

'Do not grow old, no matter how long you live. Never cease to stand like curious children before the great mystery into which we were born.'

Albert Einstein

Right then, here we go.
You made a mess of this tee shot last time.
Come on, think positive. Block out the negative thoughts.
That grip feels a bit tight. Just relax!
Visualise the shot you want to hit.
Nice and smooth, don't rush the takeaway . . .
Noooo! Not over there!
You're such an idiot!
Why did you do that?

I HAVE DISCUSSED THE MENTAL SIDE of the game with hundreds of golfers over the last twenty years. Their experiences confirm that similar unspoken conversations take place daily on golf courses all over the world.

I use the word *conversation*, but I'm not sure that's an accurate description.

A conversation is usually back and forth. An interchange of ideas. Question and response. One observation or point of view countered by or embellished with another.

These internal golf dialogues are one-way traffic. Someone seems to be talking to someone else. But there is rarely, if ever, a response.

From a cold, rational perspective, this seems odd. You probably don't run through a mental 'how to' manual or give yourself a pep talk when mowing the lawn or preparing a meal.

An internal commentary may still occur, but it's rarely instructional or even connected to what you are doing. It's often about something unrelated.

So why does a stream of advice start when we pick up a golf club? And why do we take so seriously what the voice is suggesting?

This book is an investigation of what golfers mean when they lament, *'I'm getting in my own way again.'*

Important clues can be found in the mental discourse that arises on the golf course, compared to other areas of life.

CHAPTER 1: INTRODUCTION

The Story So Far

My name is Sam Jarman. I'm a PGA golf professional and coach.

I played full-time golf for ten years as an elite amateur and for my own money on various mini tours in the UK and Europe. These days most of my time is spent sharing these ideas with coaches and athletes in different sports and organisations.

In 2015, I wrote my first book, *The Three Principles of Outstanding Golf*. It has sold thousands of copies worldwide over the past eight years. In 2019, a follow-up, *Take Relief – Uncover the Myths and Misunderstandings of Golf Performance*, was published.

Readers frequently get in touch to share their experiences and to ask questions. Some say that exploration of the ideas shared in those books has been a turning point, leading to a new approach to golf and life.

A similar change in perspective occurred in my own game. I realised that when my best golf showed up, something was different in how I experienced what was happening.

The best way I can describe it is that I was present, but 'Sam' wasn't.

This sense of detachment was a mystery at the time. I had picked up the belief that a particular mindset was necessary for me to perform to my potential. And that I needed to do something to get into that state.

I believed that focus and concentration were essential skills I needed to learn, work on, and develop. That success would come from doing more. From grinding and suffering and trying harder.

Yet, my experience was that I was only 'doing something' when I was struggling. When I was playing well, it felt like I wasn't 'doing' much of anything at all. The game seemed easy. I felt relaxed, confident and composed. There was full engagement, but without trying to concentrate or focus. The contrast with the days of directing my swing and trying to manage my thinking was stark.

But from a mindset of wanting and needing to be in control, evidence that letting go helped my performance was hard to accept.

The Problem with Golf Psychology

Coaching other golfers confirmed my suspicion that establishing a simple, functional golf swing wasn't that difficult. But trusting and repeating it was a different matter. My own experience showed that the mental side of the game was at least as important as the technical or physical aspects, but was usually overlooked.

People who came for lessons often had good skills, but when it mattered most, they weren't playing anywhere near their potential.

The frustrations I had experienced when trying to earn a living from playing the game were widely shared. Resources to help golfers understand their thoughts and feelings around the game were limited. There were anecdotes and opinions from former players and golf commentators. Or there were books by psychologists, most of whom had never played any sport at a high level.

In *Take Relief*, I described how the techniques and strategies offered by golf psychologists and performance coaches might help some people, some of the time.

But a swing thought or pre-shot routine that corresponded to a good performance one day would fail miserably next time you played. Visualising the right shot was easy in a practice round, but impossible when you were 2 down with two to play. A confident feeling one moment would dissipate without anything having changed in terms of the situation in the game.

The explanations for these experiences didn't seem to be based on logic or reason. So, in the absence of consistent outcomes, it was easier to slip back onto the endless diet of technical instruction where at least a vague correlation between a swing alteration and a change in ball flight might be apparent.

Paradoxically, the golfers I coached who improved the most seemed to be the ones who just stopped searching for solutions to their swing problems. From a traditional golf improvement perspective, they stopped trying to get better.

Staying away from the driving range and unsubscribing from the YouTube channels they were binge watching seemed to free them up.

They accepted their limitations, quit fixing their golf swings, and just played in the way that felt natural and authentic.

Playing the way they did before they started trying to become something, or someone they weren't, had a surprising effect. Their expectations dropped, consistency improved, and enjoyment of the game returned.

A Different Approach

If you have read *The Three Principles of Outstanding Golf* or *Take Relief*, or have had similar experience to the one just described, you won't be surprised that the approach I'm suggesting will be different to that promoted by the mainstream golf instruction industry.

There are no techniques or strategies to 'improve' your thinking or control emotions. I won't offer any tools, tips, or tricks, or routines to work on when you play.

CHAPTER 1: INTRODUCTION

There will be some questions to help you to look at golf from a different perspective. There will be thought experiments to encourage investigation of your current mental habits and patterns. Understanding what is happening before changing it is the logical plan of attack in my experience.

But before we go any further, I'm going to make a request. I'm assuming you want to become a better golfer or wish to fix a problem you believe is stopping you reaching your potential. This desire is probably why you picked up this book in the first place.

If you can, please just set those aspirations aside until you have finished reading. You can always come back to them later.

You have nurtured them for a long time, so a short pause is unlikely to thwart your ambitions. Think of it as taking a step back to take two forward.

Please just regard what follows as a possibility to consider. If you must have a goal, simply have an open mind to what is being suggested in these pages. It isn't a textbook or recipe book that needs to be followed step by step.

I hope the reasons for this note of caution will become clear as you progress through, but patience will help. Part One is a broad overview of why we think and feel the way we do, rather than just addressing the specific problems facing golfers.

Reading it carefully and being open to what is being suggested will make Parts Two and Three – which do directly address the issues encountered playing the game – more relatable, and hopefully more useful.

Please also be aware that the book contains only one main idea. I use several metaphors and analogies to point towards it. Your intellect may rebel against some of the repetition, as it wants to tick the box and get onto the next thing.

If you can put these dissenting thoughts to one side, grasping this singular concept will solve the challenges many golfers experience. And fully comprehending it can have an impact far beyond the game.

Who's Playing?

There's a thought expressed by frustrated golfers wherever the game is played.

Most often it is heard from people who know they can play better than they seem able to when it's most important to them.

'If only I could get out of my own way.'

Anyone who has played the game for more than a few minutes is aware that the biggest obstacle to improving and to playing your best isn't the golf course, or your golf swing, or your opponent.

CHAPTER 1: INTRODUCTION

It's the voice in your head. The one that pipes up with comments and judgements, often at the most inappropriate moment. A narrative apparently between an entity whose role seems to be assessing how well things are going, evaluating what that might mean and instructing on what to do... and another that is actually playing. The exchange at the start of the chapter is an example.

The Inner Game of Golf is one of the best-selling books on the subject. Author Timothy Gallwey labelled this voice 'Self One', and the entity to whom the voice is talking 'Self Two'.

When I read *The Inner Game* more than thirty years ago, the idea he was advancing resonated with me. But like most golfers, I couldn't get beyond the concept to investigate and grasp the relevance of this inner narrative. Where would you even begin such an enquiry?

Are there really two golfers playing? Which 'self' is the real you?

Who is getting in who's way?

Who is in charge? Is it the one doing the talking or the one listening (or being talked at?)

These questions seem like gobbledegook.

But I couldn't dismiss the tantalising possibility (and my gut feeling) that Gallwey was onto something. Could solving the riddle lead to a quieter mind, and ultimately, prevent the self-sabotage I and so many other golfers were familiar and frustrated with?

Strategy, or Superstition?

I can sympathise if you are wary of committing time, energy, and money to the mental or philosophical side of the game. Most of us have dabbled from time to time with the theories and concepts offered by well-meaning sports psychologists and mind coaches.

These theories are often based on third-party observations or anecdotal research rather than an individual golfer's own, direct experience. Practices such as visualisation or affirmations often feel like mind tricks or self-deception. A bit 'woo-woo'.

A mental technique or practice employed without evidence of consistent results or outcomes isn't a strategy. It's a superstition.

This book offers an alternative.

The available evidence will be examined to identify whom or what is issuing the instructions when you step onto the first tee. And who or what they are talking to.

Logic, reason, and rational thought will be used to weigh that evidence before accepting or rejecting it. The implications for your golf of discovering the truth about who is playing the game will be investigated.

Truth is powerful because it immediately allows the elimination of complications and distractions. A simplification of life and of the way you play the game of golf automatically follows.

This means having less to worry about, less to think about. Less on your mind.

You play more instinctively and with more freedom, creativity, and confidence.

You stop getting in your own way.

Let's make a start.

A Simple Thought Experiment

To begin our enquiry, take a moment to think about the following question:

What would change if you set aside all the things you think of as *belonging* to you, but *that aren't really you?* For example:

The voice in your head.

Your mind.

Your body.

Your beliefs.

Your thoughts.

Your personality.

Your feelings.

Your perceptions.

Your memories.

What would life (and golf) be like without all this mental baggage?

Without the judgements and expectations that come along with an identity.

What would remain if you dropped the attachment to these ideas?

Would you still be *you*?

Key Points and Questions from Chapter 1:
- Most golfers have an internal dialogue when they play. But have you ever really investigated the nature of that conversation?
- Have you ever 'given up' on the golf course? Or had a break from taking lessons or stopped trying to improve? What happened?
- When a golfer says, "'I' am getting in my own way," who or what is the impediment? Who or what is being impeded?
- Write down a list of the labels you use to describe yourself, or the roles you define yourself with? Would you still be *'you'* if the labels changed or disappeared?

CHAPTER 2

Learn Something

'The best thing for being sad, replied Merlin, beginning to puff and blow, is to learn something. That's the only thing that never fails.

You may grow old and trembling in your anatomies, you may lie awake at night listening to the disorder of your veins, you may miss your only love, you may see the world about you devastated by evil lunatics, or know your honour trampled in the sewers of baser minds.

There is only one thing for it then – to learn. Learn why the world wags and what wags it.'

T. H. White, *The Once and Future King*

WE'VE ALL BEEN THERE. Walking down the 17th fairway frustrated and fed up.

Handicap blown in the first eight holes. Since then, it has been damage limitation.

You just want to get back to the clubhouse with the last of your dignity and the same number of clubs in the same number of pieces as when you stepped onto the first tee.

Your playing partners will ask you to stay for a drink. But what you really want to do is throw the bag in the car boot and get the hell out of there.

You were really looking forward to the round. That's the disappointing bit.

Practice on the range with that new swing thought was going well.

The consistent strike and ball flight suggested that today would be the day when it all fell into place.

But somehow the feeling just wasn't there when you got to the first tee.

The harder you tried, the worse it got. Back-to-back double bogeys on 5 and 6 pretty much finished you off.

So here you are. All over again. Trudging down to your usual bay with a large bucket of balls.

Back at square one.

Fed up and confused.

It's Not in the Dirt

When I was playing tournaments, experiences like the one described above were not unfamiliar.

My default response to a bad day was to work harder, to figure it out. To read a golf book or have a lesson. To analyse what had gone wrong and to fix it.

Logically, I knew that for suffering to end, something needed to change.

For change to occur, I needed to learn something.

It looked like a golf problem. So, a golf solution was what I sought.

I would go to the range or to the putting green. Hit some balls or work on my stroke. Maybe a new swing thought or an insight would come along. I'd feel like I had discovered something, solved a problem. Got back on track.

A little spark of hope would flicker into a flame. I'd look forward to testing whatever it was in the next round. And so, the pattern would continue.

To experiment and innovate seems to be a human instinct. Learning is intrinsically satisfying. Excitement arises from understanding something we didn't before. A sense of accomplishment or closure follows if the insight has solved a particular problem. We will explore the desire for certainty and control in a later chapter.

This response to a setback is better than some alternatives, like drowning your sorrows at the 19th hole or buying yet another piece of expensive technology. But it can become another form of addiction. Knowledge accumulates. But you remain stuck if what is learnt doesn't address what is getting in the way.

Being a fast runner is a mixed blessing if you have no sense of direction. Being a good learner is only an asset if you can distinguish between information that is valuable and important, and what is interesting but irrelevant.

As many people have discovered, golf can be a source of endless fascination. The game has so many different parts. You can occupy yourself for a lifetime trying to perfect them all.

The recent availability of accurate statistics has helped golfers to analyse their strengths and weaknesses, and to train more efficiently. The numbers prove that some aspects of the game – such as driving the ball straight and far, holing out from close range – are disproportionally important compared to shots you don't encounter very often. Like escaping from a plugged lie in a bunker, or playing a flop shot from hardpan.

The logic of Pareto's law suggests that spending hours practicing shots you rarely face isn't an efficient use of your time. Improving and polishing fundamentals of the game encountered in every round would be better for your scores.

Most golfers will be familiar with the pattern of finding the fairways but missing the greens with approach shots. The frustration of hitting irons well but not holing enough putts. The heartache of playing well for fifteen holes, then blowing up on the last three.

CHAPTER 2: LEARN SOMETHING

Something always seems to prevent it all coming together. If only you could learn how to nail it down at the same time. Find a way to cut out the silly mistakes.

Once I stopped playing tournaments, my coaching career has been a quest to find out why some golfers (starting with the one I know best) don't improve beyond a certain level. Why do we feel our potential hasn't been reached, despite improving our swings and gaining more and more knowledge about how to play the game?

Like many golfers, you probably take lessons, update your equipment, read golf instruction magazines or books, follow your favourite YouTube gurus and go to the driving range.

But since that initial surge of improvement from novice to actual golfer, I'll bet your scores have stayed pretty much in the same range despite all the effort and time trying to improve. It seems that a law of diminishing returns has greater effect as a golfer's handicap comes down.

Why is this? I'm sure it has puzzled and frustrated other coaches too. It's only recently that I have come to understand the key reason why golfers fail to reach their potential.

And it isn't a golf problem.

What I needed to learn most was never going to be found by digging in the dirt.

How Change Happens

When a problem arises that seems difficult or impossible to solve, it's usually because you're asking the wrong question.

If you ask a different question or frame the problem in a different way, it disappears or the solution becomes obvious.

In order to learn what we need to learn, maybe golfers need to ask different questions? Ones that aren't narrowly focused around the technicalities of hitting a ball with a stick.

How do behaviour changes occur in other areas of life?

What causes a smoker to drop a 40-a-day habit?

Why does someone finally walk out of a dysfunctional relationship after decades of unhappiness?

What causes someone to shed half their body weight and start doing triathlons after years of a sedentary lifestyle?

These things happen. My question is: *why do they happen?*

The answer is obvious when I reflect on my own experience.

Looking at the way my life has unfolded over the past fifteen years, hindsight shows that the most significant changes have come when, after many years of believing something, I finally realised that it wasn't true.

Or vice versa.

Three significant realisations stand out.

The first was the belief that how many over par I was, the importance of the tournament, or my standing on an order of merit was the cause of how I felt on the golf course. I realised that my thinking in the moment affected my state of mind far more that what was happening, on or off the fairways.

This had profound implications for my golf and for other areas of my life, as described in my previous books.

The second big insight was recognising and accepting that I have no choice about what I think or when I think it. Therefore, control over my state of mind and the behaviour that arises from it, is an illusion.

If didn't know what I would be thinking in a moments time, how could I know how I would feel then?

I might be in a low mood now, but in a few minutes I could be happy and loving life.

One fresh thought could change everything.

The Problem with Willpower

Most people believe their thoughts and feelings are caused by what is going on outside of them. Yet at the same time they are very attached to the idea that they are (or should be) in control of what they think, feel, and do in the world.

Can you see the contradiction?

When you believe something that isn't true, your gut instinct, inner wisdom or whatever you want to call it, lets you know. Anxious, uneasy, insecure feelings arise. What happens next depends on how you interpret these feelings.

If you believe that you are in control, that you have agency over your thinking and behaviour, then it will make sense to use willpower or 'strength of mind' to push yourself into doing what, from a place of insecurity and doubt, you think you *should* be doing.

It isn't hard to anticipate the problems with this approach. For starters, huge amount of extra thinking and mental effort is required. We call the feeling associated with this exertion 'stress'.

Trying to overcome a belief that is false by repeatedly telling yourself that it is true is extremely hard work, and usually the pretence can only be maintained for a limited time.

You might win the odd skirmish with reality, but in the long run there is only one victor.

A Simple Solution?

I've never met anyone who enjoys being depressed. Not many people are happy doing jobs they dislike, being smokers, being in toxic relationships, having the chipping yips, or searching for their ball in the right-hand rough every time they play.

Telling people that they have a choice and that they can or should control these behaviours – or change them – doesn't seem to be working, and probably never will.

If it was as simple as choosing not to, why do we see so many examples of dissatisfaction and unhappiness?

Asking or telling someone to fix their behaviour is the opposite of what will help them. It fortifies the false belief in control. Thinking revs up and they feel worse.

When they feel worse, they are more likely to carry on. Or revert to familiar habits to distract themselves or compensate. They head to the bar, or to the fridge, to the television, or to the driving range. They have direct evidence from experience that relief can be found here. At least in the short term.

My response to a bad round was to ask: What do I need to fix in my golf to avoid feeling how I'm feeling now? I'd get a large bucket of practice balls and hope to find an answer by the time I got to the bottom of it.

There was always the possibility of an insight, an aha moment, a new feeling. Such a moment of understanding brings the seeking to an end – for a while.

Rather than dwelling on what had gone wrong, my thinking moved on to a possibly better future.

The pain and frustration began to ease.

Looking back, it's obvious this behaviour was a coping mechanism rather than a coherent strategy to realise my potential as a golfer. But that was the culture and the reality I lived in.

Millions of people are trapped in a similar cycle, asking the wrong questions, then trying to fix their life situation to gain some relief from the suffering.

The Role of a Coach

I realised a while ago that I can't make anyone do something if they don't want to do it. Or teach them something if they want to learn about something else. The only way anyone makes a change is through having an insight. Through realising that something is true.

Or seeing that something they believed to be true actually isn't. By living more in harmony with reality rather than constantly fighting it.

CHAPTER 2: LEARN SOMETHING

A coach can help by provoking your intellect – your logical, rational mind – to explore your beliefs about yourself, your golf, and your assumptions about how the world works.

Sometimes in this collaboration, an insight occurs. There is recognition that a strongly held belief isn't based on the evidence of experience.

When such an insight arises, willpower, control or self-deception aren't necessary for change to occur. Thinking calms down, and the mind clears, leaving room for more insights to flow.

When insight flows, we see more clearly what is and isn't true about life and about ourselves.

It becomes a virtuous circle. Our perception of the world aligns more closely with the reality of it.

Rather than reinforcing the belief that a cigarette, or a chocolate bar, or another beer, or holing 100 three-footers in a row will make things better, such impulses aren't taken seriously, if they are even noticed at all.

Rather than indulging the thought that going for a run will be painful or uncomfortable, you get outside and find yourself jogging along. At some point there is pleasant surprise when you realise you're enjoying the fresh air, and you feel even better afterwards.

You're shelling another large bucket of balls

down the driving range trying to cure that slice, when a straight shot occurs. An insight pops up suggesting what might have occurred differently in the swing to change the ball flight. A few more shots with the same feeling and you're no longer a slicer!

This is how significant change happens on a deep and sustainable level. Suddenly, you become aware that habitual and intractable behaviour just somehow isn't happening.

Previous beliefs about good, bad, right, and wrong don't make sense anymore. They aren't dispelled through coercion or willpower. It happens through insight. When a belief ends, it no longer occurs to go back to a previous pattern of thinking and behaviour.

Context is Key

The fact that I can't teach anyone anything is one of the most important things I've learned about being a coach. All I can do is point towards what is true and hope that someone suspends their current beliefs for a moment to allow a new perspective to arise.

This happens when you ask someone a different question than the ones they've been asking themselves.

What I'm suggesting in the coming pages will contrast with most modern golf instruction. We are absorbing more and more information about golf and golf swings. But the average handicap hasn't improved over the last forty years.

The problem is that all information is contextual. An observation or event that means one thing from one perspective can mean something completely different when observed from another.

So, if you don't understand the context, your understanding of the object or event will be limited.

Any information you become aware of in the context of learning golf will be filtered and absorbed through your pre-conceived notions about how life works and, crucially, about who you think you are. What the game means to you will also be influenced by these beliefs.

We all know golfers who could write a book about the golf swing but can't break 90. In the realm of intellectual knowledge, describing the game, they might be experts. But in the context of building and performing functional movement patterns and shooting a score, they are novices.

No matter how much information you have, you can't understand the view until you understand the nature of the window through which you are perceiving it.

In the next chapter, we will explore in detail the nature of our window on the world – our beliefs. How and why they change, and the consequences unrecognised biases and assumptions can have on your golf.

We will also have an initial look at the third of the big realisations that had a profound impact on my golf and my life.

Key Points and Questions from Chapter 2:

- Learning and improving are an inherent aspect of the game. But are we neglecting the most important lessons?
- Are you making the progress anticipated? If not, are you asking the wrong questions?
- Have you ever fixed something in your game, only for something else to go wrong next time you play? Why do you think that pattern occurs?
- Have you ever let go of a strongly held belief? What happened?
- What was the catalyst for questioning that belief?

CHAPTER 3

The Problem of Belief

I don't want to believe; I want to know.

Carl Sagan

BEFORE YOU CAN FEEL DIFFERENTLY ABOUT SOMETHING, a change in thinking or perspective occurs.

But sometimes it's hard to give yourself intellectual permission to challenge long-standing beliefs, especially when they are constantly reinforced by society. But often, the misconceptions that you take for granted are the very things that obstruct the path to the golf you are capable of and restrict your enjoyment of your game.

As I hope was made clear in the previous chapter, if there is an intention behind this book, it's to encourage you to ask some different questions about yourself, about golf, and about life. In my experience, when you understand something fully, the urge to fix or correct it often goes away.

Belief is usually defined as:

Confidence in the truth or existence of something not

immediately susceptible to rigorous proof.

If the goal is to move towards greater understanding, there is no point in simply replacing one set of superstitions with another set. As philosopher Socrates observed centuries ago, false beliefs are more damaging than no beliefs at all.

I encourage you to test your current beliefs and theories about golf against the ideas that I will propose. There will be thought experiments along the way to help you do so.

The aim is to move past belief. To uncover a philosophy that informs the way we play based on what we know to be true rather than on hearsay or habit.

Beyond the Game

To break free from assumptions and patterns of thinking acquired from our golfing culture, I suggest we first need to investigate our ideas about reality and about the nature of our experience *prior to* and *beyond* the game.

After all, golf doesn't exist in a vacuum. It is governed by the laws of nature and subject to the influences of wider society and culture. Looking at golf in isolation would be like a biologist studying an organism with no consideration of the environment in which it lives. You cannot understand behaviour without context.

CHAPTER 3: THE PROBLEM OF BELIEF

Exploring the nature of reality and the place and meaning of human life within it might sound like a daunting and arduous task. But fortunately, we have been blessed with a powerful mental apparatus that will assist the analysis and reasoning.

The mind is an amazing tool. Perhaps uniquely among species, we have developed self-awareness, the capacity for *conscious metacognition*.

We experience, and we are also aware *that* we experience.

Here is a simple example: Right now, are you breathing?

A few seconds ago, you were having the experience of air coming into your lungs and being exhaled, but you were probably not *meta* consciously aware of it. You were absorbed in reading or listening to these words.

When I asked the question, you noticed your breath flowing in and out through your nose or mouth and your chest and belly expanding and contracting. You became aware that you were aware of the sensations.

We constantly have thoughts and experiences of which we are unaware or barely aware. But we can also focus upon, analyse and interrogate our experience. We can examine ideas and beliefs and compare them with alternatives. We can contemplate the past and imagine the future.

This ability to self-reflect allows us to use logic and reason to investigate our environment, both the internal and external contexts of our lives. (Unfortunately, this enhancement in our mental functioning comes at a cost, as we will see in a later chapter.)

We can detect and observe the patterns and regularities of the world around us. We can accurately predict how nature will behave. This in turn allows us to develop technologies that transform the way we live.

Many of us are lucky enough to experience levels of safety and comfort in our societies that our ancestors could not even dream about. These advancements have transpired through use of the scientific method, a framework that allows us to interrogate reality in a way that makes reliance on beliefs increasingly unnecessary.

A hypothesis (a scientific term for a belief) is framed in terms of a question. An experiment is conducted to test the hypothesis. Nature responds with an answer. The hypothesis (belief) is proved or disproved. Logic and reason are employed to interpret the outcome and consider the implications. A new hypothesis is framed, and the process continues.

Direct experience of reality (empirical evidence or rigorous proof) gained through experimentation

CHAPTER 3: THE PROBLEM OF BELIEF

makes belief an option rather than a necessity.

The Most Cherished Belief

Uncovering the truth of something is a process of stripping away existing beliefs, theories, and ideologies rather than adding new information.

Most important discoveries are simplifications rather than expansions of information and complexity. Einstein's general theory of relativity, perhaps the most significant realignment of our belief in how the universe works, can be described in a simple one-line equation.

$E=mc^2$

One parsimonious mathematical statement allowed theories and beliefs about the nature of reality that had influenced behaviour for hundreds of years to be discarded.

We all have a set of concepts and mental models that inform the way we live our lives and play golf. Some are informed by direct experience. But many are not. These underlying beliefs give rise to our habits and patterns of thinking that arise in the moment. Our behaviour is largely a result of this thinking.

If you are like most people, your most fundamental and deeply-held belief is the story of who you think you are.

You have a description of how you arrived here, about your destiny, how your character was formed, why your personality is how it is. A constantly updating narrative about your strengths, your weaknesses, your preferences, your fears, your relationships.

You will have some theories about how certain events along the way affected who you are now, and probably some ideas about what might help you to become the person you really want to be.

This mental model and how it relates to other beliefs provides a behavioural framework that allows us to survive and play in the environment we experience.

Most of us are very attached to the story of who we think we are, to the extent we take belief in it for granted. This attachment has consequences, both at a personal level and for our societies and civilisations.

Sadly, throughout human history, wars have been fought and millions of lives lost over strongly held beliefs or concepts of identity. One story about relationships and traditions is pitched against another, and violence ensues.

Peace only comes when beliefs are changed or compromised.

What Do You Know for Sure?

We all have beliefs once held very dear that we now see are not true, and never were. This retrospection often occurs in the face of considerable suffering. Suffering is what we feel when our cherished ideas and reality collide.

What causes us to have a change of mind, leading to a change of heart? A genuine transformation in how we feel about or understand something.

In almost all cases, it happens when a belief is confronted by the undeniable evidence of your own direct experience.

By 'experience', I don't mean the sum of memories and knowledge you might have accumulated over the years. Your theory or story about what is going on.

By 'experience', I mean evidence, *rigorous proof* of what is true. Right here, right now.

By definition, a belief isn't based on evidence. And annoyingly, our capacity to think about our thinking, that which makes us adaptive, also allows us to deceive ourselves.

This creates a dilemma. What can we trust? What can we rely on?

On closer examination, it becomes apparent that our concepts of who we are and about reality itself are not based on the evidence of experience. No wonder so many people feel lost and insecure so much of the time. We bring this insecurity into our activities and relationships.

Golf is no exception.

The Alternative

Let's try to stabilise these shaky foundations by at least clearly understanding the problem. We can start by restating the alternatives described in the previous paragraphs.

Which is more reliable, belief, or your experience?

It seems to me the answer is simple.

All that is known, or could ever be known, is your *direct experience.*

Experience alone must be the test of what we take reality to be. Even a belief is *experienced* as a thought, or a framework of thoughts.

If we ignore the evidence of what our direct experience is telling us, then belief is the only alternative.

You have been confronted with this dilemma many times in your life. When you have overcome something challenging or taken a step towards understanding, it's always when you accepted the evidence rather than preferring your beliefs.

Something unexpected happens. A surprising event occurs that challenges your assumptions. As a result, something new was seen that suggested what you previously thought or believed can't be accepted any more. It wasn't true.

We have all had this happen on the putting green. The putt looks like it breaks left, so you aim an inch outside the right edge of the cup.

The ball starts along the line, but it curves to the right.

The belief that the slope went from right to left was wrong. The belief has been disproved by experience.

Many golfers who slice believe that the ball ends up missing the fairway because the clubface is open to the target at impact.

But this often turns out not to be the case when they hit shots on a launch monitor and confirm the impact factors.

The clubface is pointing left of the target. But the swing path is going even further to the left, imparting sidespin. Hence the ball curving off and missing the fairway to the right. (The reverse being true for the left-handed).

Unless you know what is really happening – what is true – changing your ball flight and correcting the predominant shot pattern is a challenge because the struggle is with a different problem than what you believed it to be.

Reality wasn't wrong. Your perception and interpretation of it was. Your belief was based on a misunderstanding. A more accurate interpretation of reality allows your behaviour to change.

The Problem with Self-Belief

Nowhere is the problem with belief more relevant than the issue of self-belief.

Most of us have been told from a young age that 'self-belief' is something we must have. That successful people have lots of it and – if it's something that we, or someone else has decided that we lack – it needs to be nurtured and developed.

What is this 'self' that we are supposed to believe in?

As described earlier, most people identify as the central character in the story of their lives. But we have already established that the story of 'who you think you are', is a mishmash of memories, theories, assumptions, ambitions, etc. A conceptualisation for which evidence or rigorous proof is lacking.

In other words, another belief.

So, when someone suggests that more 'self-belief' is required, what they are really suggesting is that you need to have more belief in another belief.

I'm not sure how this is supposed to be helpful.

If you are the central character in the story of you,

who or what knows the story, who is aware of it?

Which of these 'selves' are we supposed to believe in? We are back to the conundrum described by Tim Gallwey over fifty years ago.

The True Nature of Experience

All that we know, all that we could ever really know, is experience.

Direct experience is the only laboratory available for our enquiries into the truth about reality, about the game of golf, and about ourselves. If something exists outside awareness, outside of consciousness, we can have no knowledge of it.

Therefore, we cannot say anything about it.

It isn't an experience.

We can have a belief about it, but we can't *know* it as truth.

Have you ever experienced anything outside your experience, outside of awareness?

In order to know a thing you weren't aware of, something would need to be aware of the fact you weren't aware of it.

So, you can't even be unaware without being aware of it.

Awareness is the primary element of our experience, and as such, understanding the nature of awareness, or consciousness, is the most important knowledge you can ever have.

It is the knowledge that underpins knowledge of everything else.

It is the window through which everything in our lives is viewed.

It is the only thing a human being can know for certain. It is the *only* thing we know to be true. As French philosopher René Descartes famously put it,

Cogito, ergo sum.

I know, therefore I am.

This is the one big idea we will explore in the chapters that follow.

The nature of awareness (and therefore *your* true nature) is the starting point if we really want to understand golf, work, life, relationships, and everything else.

On every page of the book, keep the following question in the back of your mind:

What is more trustworthy – beliefs, or your experience brought to you via awareness?

And what does experience tell you about the following question:

Who are you? Is it who you believe yourself to be?

CHAPTER 3: THE PROBLEM OF BELIEF

By examining the implications of these questions in the contexts of creativity, confidence, consistency, concentration, and composure, you can move closer to the truth about how your experience of golf and life really works.

The more you understand the true nature of awareness, of consciousness, the better you understand your experience, and the better you understand your reasons for playing the game and the feelings associated with it.

In the next chapter, we'll explore a belief I doubt many golfers have examined, but is highly relevant if we are to understand our experience of the game in the wider context of our lives:

What is the fundamental nature of the environment in which we live – and in which the game we love is played?

Key Points from Chapter 3:
- Replacing one set of beliefs for which you have no evidence with another set isn't progress.
- There is a difference between consciousness (awareness), and metacognition (self-awareness).
- Metacognition is the mental faculty that allows us to question our beliefs.
- The most significant unexamined belief held by most people is the belief in who they are.
- The only thing you know for certain is that you are aware. You can test this at any time.

CHAPTER 4

Mind Over Golf

'The moment you change your perception is the moment you rewrite the chemistry of your body.'

Dr Bruce H Lipton

OUR WESTERN CULTURE, and therefore the subculture in which golf is played, is grounded in the belief that reality is made up of two clearly defined constituents – matter and mind.

This manifests as distinction between the physical game (swing, putting stroke, short game, athleticism, technique, and golf equipment) and the mental or inner game (thinking, feeling, remembering, imagining, and decision-making).

In almost all aspects of life, matter – the stuff we can apparently measure, touch, feel, see, buy, and own – is considered the primary element.

It is widely believed that the physical world arrived first and that it gives rise to our subjective experience – to our thoughts and feelings. Consciousness emanates from your brain, which is made of matter. Stubbing your toe on a rock causes discomfort. Owning a house makes you feel secure. Money in your pocket gives you freedom. Winning a match makes you feel confident. Hitting a straight, solid 2-iron onto the green of a long par 4 brings satisfaction.

This belief dictates the priorities when we are learning golf. The physical elements of the game are deemed more significant and therefore given more attention than the mental. How many hours have you spent working on your swing compared to understanding the thoughts and feelings that arise when you play?

Yet, many elite-level players have reflected that it should be the other way round. The more proficient at striking and controlling the flight of the ball you are, the more important the mental game becomes.

Unfortunately, this important message doesn't seem to influence golfers' behaviour at any level of the game.

Most of us spend far more time, money, and effort learning and developing our 'outer game' than we do understanding how our minds really work. Learning about the process through which subjective experience of the game of golf is created is very much an afterthought.

If indeed it is considered at all.

CHAPTER 4: MIND OVER GOLF

A Brief History Lesson

So, the way reality is perceived by most people is that everything is made or derived from this physical substance called 'matter'. Philosophers sometimes describe this worldview as the 'materialist paradigm'.

According to this model, matter came into existence around fourteen billion years ago. Exactly how is not yet fully explained. The fundamental elements of it are often characterised as 'the building blocks of the universe'. They are identified and described in the Standard Model of particle physics – electrons, protons, neutrons, etc.

The golf courses we walk on, and the clubs, balls, and other equipment used also consist of matter. They seem to be tangible and solid. Made from something real, substantial, stable, and well defined. The discovery that according to this *very same model of reality*, this solidity, this tangibility, and stability is an illusion – is therefore a surprise.

In this paradigm, consciousness (or mind), as the aware element of our experience, is also a *derivative* of matter. It is assumed that somehow, awareness emanates from a particular arrangement or activity of the subatomic particles from which the brains and other physiology of sentient beings is composed.

The causal process by which this occurs is regarded as a mystery that scientists still haven't solved after 300 years of investigation. In his 1996 book, *The Conscious Mind*, philosopher David Chalmers frames this lack of a coherent explanation for how electrochemical activity in brain cells gives rise to subjective experience, as the 'hard problem of consciousness'.

As of today, there is no plausible theory for the mechanism by which the awareness of the blueness of blue, the taste of chocolate, or the pain of a toothache arises from brain tissues. Most of a brain is made from water. At what point after you drink it this water learns to think is unclear.

A theory for this confusion about the relationship between the brain and our knowing of experience is revealed if we take a brief look at the history of science.

In the late fifteenth century, interest in the organised study of nature was growing. This was a positive development in many fields, allowing the development of technologies that we are still benefitting from today.

Unfortunately, there was a problem when it came to investigating the human mind and body. At the time, the church, particularly the Catholic church, was perhaps the most powerful organisation in the western world. It protected its interests and influence with zeal.

As far as the church was concerned the human soul or 'psyche' was off limits for these new studies.

Questioning or contradicting established religious teachings regarding the nature of human beings and their thoughts, feelings, and behaviours was a risky business.

So, to create a safe space where science could be practiced without fear of a knock on the door from the Inquisition, a social and political divide was created between the physical and the mental. Between the material and the spiritual.

As part of the 'physical' world, the body was available for study and research by science. Mind and spirit were territory jealously guarded by the church.

This belief in the separation between the body and subjective experience is an artifact that unfortunately still prevails in many scientific and medical communities.

The reasons for it were justified at the time, but the unforeseen side effects have been disastrous. We are suffering the consequences of that legacy to this day.

This is the background against which the greatest intellects of our recent history have proposed several theories about the origins of consciousness. But thus far (unsurprisingly, given the premise on which they are based) none have been proven.

Due to a historical mistake early in the chain of

reasoning, there is a particular lack of evidence supporting the theory that consciousness, and therefore subjective experience, somehow springs forth from the matter comprising the human brain.

Yet this does not seem to deter most branches of science or the scientists who work in them from adhering to the materialist paradigm.

In most fields of scientific research, the absence of evidence for the basic premise on which a theory is founded would be enough for it to be treated with suspicion.

But when it comes to matter and consciousness, most scientists persist with the belief that a few more years and a few more billion dollars in funding will uncover the proof they have been searching for:

Evidence that consciousness somehow springs forth from physicality. From this substance called matter, yet to be proved to exist.

A Failing Paradigm?

Given the success of science in developing technologies, the role that those technologies play in modern life, and the platform given to scientists in academia and the media, it shouldn't be a surprise that acceptance of the material model is prevalent, almost universal.

It is understandable then, that the world of golf,

particularly golf instruction, is also reluctant to venture outside the materialist paradigm. Few other sports have been changed by science and technology in the way that golf has been over the past 70 years or so.

Millions of dollars have been invested in research, manufacturing and marketing of golf equipment, swing analysis tools, training and practice aids, and health and fitness products for golfers.

Despite this investment in making the game easier to learn and play, the average handicap remains stuck around the 16 mark. Participation levels in established golf markets are static if not falling. Many golfers are not really improving, and they don't seem to be enjoying the game much more than their predecessors.

Rather than continuing on the current path, maybe we need to ask a different question.

Could the frustration and dissatisfaction that so many golfers experience stem from a misunderstanding more significant than simple failure to grasp the physics and biomechanics of the game?

Could it be that the struggles facing golfers – and those facing wider society – have their roots in a failing and outdated belief about the fundamental nature of reality?

Let's see if we can frame the issue in a way to

make consideration of it a practical matter, rather than theoretical.

The ultimate reality of the universe is what it is – regardless of our theories about it.

Indeed for most people, the difference of one model versus another seems esoteric, irrelevant. The influence of what reality is on the day-to-day activity of earning a living, raising a family, and enjoying limited free time and hobbies is not obvious.

Most golfers just want to live their lives and enjoy the game. Discussion of an abstract topic that our culture regards as settled and has taken for granted is not a priority.

But the legitimacy of the materialist paradigm has been questioned more frequently and rigorously in recent years (ironically due in part to advancements in the field of quantum mechanics). It is becoming increasingly apparent that the dissatisfaction and meaninglessness many in society are suffering with can be traced back to an unfounded belief in the material nature of reality.

This misunderstanding about reality is the reason for the exploitation and degradation of our environment. And for the widespread suspicion and animosity felt among individuals, societies, races, and nations. It is the primary cause of the inequality, division and conflict unfolding in the world today.

And for the internal division and mental conflict many golfers experience, as described in the opening paragraphs of this book.

If you think the world around you is limited and finite, and you are separate from it and from others, the pressure is on to grab as much stuff as you can before somebody else beats you to it and leaves you without.

This belief is the basis of our economic and political models.

If you believe yourself to be limited and finite, then the clock is ticking. The pressure is on to satisfy your needs and desires. To become something or someone, to make your mark. To leave a legacy before you disappear back into the primordial soup of particles and waves of energy from which you emerged.

This is the recipe for happiness and fulfilment promoted by our education systems and the media.

These unwritten, largely unexamined beliefs provide the backdrop to modern life. They underpin our values as societies, and from these values we attempt to derive meaning in our personal lives.

No wonder so many people feel stressed and under pressure. No wonder happiness and wellbeing are elusive for so many.

We turn to sport and games to try to find relief

from the struggles of the working week. But then we find that we are playing the game according to the same rules as we have imposed on ourselves in other areas of life.

No wonder enjoyment from a simple round of golf seems so elusive sometimes.

The Meaning of the Game

Compared to the challenges facing many in society, your personal quest to get a small white ball into a hole in the ground could be regarded as trivial.

But the frustration and lack of satisfaction felt by many golfers could also be a prompt to take a closer look.

Those feelings point to the misunderstanding about the ultimate nature of the human experience. And many have a suspicion that the game offers an opportunity to learn something important beyond the immediate task of finding the fairways and greens and holing more putts.

Would it not make the investment of all that time, and effort, and money more worthwhile if our quest to play better golf, also revealed something valuable about ourselves and our fellow golfers?

Something that helps make our whole life experience richer, happier, and more fulfilling.

For as long as we seek peace and happiness in the

form of achievement and attainment, the best we can hope for are brief moments of relief from an ongoing struggle.

Despite advances in club and ball technology, improved agronomy, and more information and data about how we interact with both club and ball, playing your best golf isn't a regular experience for the average golfer.

Is the game any more satisfying or fulfilling than it was for previous generations?

Maybe the remedy is more fundamental than a simplification of the rulebook, a reassessment of the technology, and yet another marketing strategy aimed at 'growing the game'.

Maybe it isn't the game of golf that needs to change. Maybe it's our beliefs about reality, about ourselves, and about what a successful life entails, that underlie the problems golf seems to be struggling with.

Hope that this change is coming might seem optimistic. Naïve even. But if we take another look at history, precedents exist.

A 'Paradigm Shift'

Over the last couple of centuries there have been many examples where revision of a long-standing belief about how the world really is has changed the course of human history.

The Structure of Scientific Revolutions, by Thomas S. Kuhn, is regarded by many scientists and philosophers as one of the most important books of the twentieth century. (It was Kuhn who first coined the ubiquitous and often misused term that I've adopted as the subheading for these paragraphs.)

The commonly held view of science (unsurprisingly not challenged by most scientists and their supporters in the media) is that the last three centuries have been a steady and relentless progression towards greater knowledge and understanding of ourselves and the universe we live in.

Kuhn clinically and systematically dismantles this interpretation of history. We have been mistaken about how things really are for decades, sometimes centuries. Every now and then a discovery is made that means much of what we think we know needs to be revised or discarded.

Science is forced to retrace its steps to where it went off track and start over in the light of the new information. These are the 'paradigm shifts' as defined by Kuhn.

The realisation that the earth is round, not flat, was one such occurrence. The discovery that the earth moved around the sun, not vice versa, was another. The transition from Newtonian physics to the theories of Einstein. From Einstein to the weird

CHAPTER 4: MIND OVER GOLF

and barely relatable world of Niels Bohr and quantum mechanics.

The fact is, science has been spectacularly wrong about a lot of things for a lot of the time. In all cases, beliefs that had served the evolution of humanity up to a point became shackles by which it was held back and prevented from evolving further.

Gradually, as the new evidence became more widely accepted, the old models were replaced by new, more accurate ones. That hundreds of years passed before they were completely accepted gives you some idea of how deeply old paradigms are woven into the psyches of the people and into the workings of societies.

The further you look back in history, the clearer it becomes that the mainstream cultural view of what reality is and how it works is usually wrong.

Why are we so certain that the current explanation is correct?

The speed with which new ideas can now be propagated and shared gives hope that overcoming the misunderstanding of the materialist paradigm will happen more quickly than the assumptions and beliefs of the past.

It is a model that served a purpose but whose usefulness has long since passed.

For the sake of golf and the people who love it,

and for the sake of the planet on which we play, I hope that this is the case.

An alternative model of reality is available. It overcomes the failings of the materialist paradigm and offers hope for a better way of living and playing.

It isn't new. Variations have been around for thousands of years and it is the foundation of the major philosophies, religions, and spiritual traditions.

This 'idea of the world' and its potential to revolutionise your golf is what we will be exploring in the rest of the book.

Key Points from Chapter 4:
- Our culture is grounded in the assumption that there is separation between the mental and the physical. And that physicality is primary.
- This distinction between mind and matter is a historical artifact, not a truth based on evidence.
- It is a major reason for many of the problems faced by society.
- Golf is not immune to the consequences of this misunderstanding. As many have found – just playing better won't necessarily improve your relationship with the game.
- There is an alternative viewpoint from which to play – as we shall uncover.

CHAPTER 5

The One, Single Cause of Pressure

'Everything changes once we identify with being the witness to the story instead of the actor in it.'

Ram Dass

LET'S PAUSE FOR A MOMENT to summarise the thread of reasoning followed so far.

In Chapter 1, we acknowledged the internal dialogue that most golfers are familiar with. Could understanding the *nature* of that narrative – investigating who is talking to whom, help us enjoy a better experience of the game instead of analysing and trying to change the *content?*

In Chapter 2, we explored the intuition that learning and understanding something new is a logical step towards playing better. But does acquiring more and more information about golf deliver long-term fulfilment and satisfaction?

If not, or if satisfaction is temporary, perhaps asking who is playing rather than constantly learning and relearning the game might be a more productive approach.

Chapter 3 identified a cause of frustration felt by many golfers. Instead of examining and trusting our own direct experience, we innocently subscribe to beliefs acquired from our prevailing culture and from other golfers – despite the lack of evidence supporting those beliefs.

And in Chapter 4, it was suggested that one fundamental belief – an outdated and disproven model of reality – could be the primary obstacle preventing many golfers from exploring who they really are and realising their potential.

In the chapters that follow, I will explain why these philosophical questions are important for golfers. How understanding the true nature of experience might help get your handicap moving in the right direction. How some deeper thinking could help you overcome the challenge of improving and allow you to enjoy your game more often.

What Might this Mean for Me?

When I speak to groups of golfers or coaches, I usually begin by summarising the current state of the game as I see it. I outline the challenges faced by golfers in the way I have tried to do thus far.

Typically, there are some nods of agreement and requests to clarify key points, suggesting that the dots are being connected.

But then comes a pause. And then, invariably, an exchange like this:

OK, Sam, I can see that the current culture around learning and playing the game isn't conducive to either performance or enjoyment.

But . . . how do we change it?

What they are really asking is

If you're right, what might this mean for me?

Well, this is the crux of the matter. A variant of the question that holds the key to understanding the way you experience the game of golf.

It shows up in many different guises, dozens of times every day. It is a query that underpins every internal dialogue, every struggle that we face both on and off the golf course.

This question may well have contributed to human beings evolving to become the most successful species on the planet. The reasons why will become clear as we explore the ideas I have shared so far in more depth.

Survival of the Most Aware

Back in Chapter 3, I suggested that our capacity for conscious metacognition – the ability to think about our thoughts and perceptions, to self-reflect – is the aspect of our mentality that sets us apart from other species. It affords human beings a significant evolutionary advantage.

What might this mean for me? is a basic example of that capability. The ability to perceive our environment, ask this question, make a judgement then act on it, and to do this quickly and efficiently has been a key factor in our domination of the planet.

The ability to reflect on our memories, to imagine the future, to predict patterns and regularities in nature, to recognise habits and biases in our own thinking and behaviour, and to make symbol associations allowing communication through language has given us a huge advantage over creatures who seem not to have developed those abilities to the same level.

Of all these facets, perhaps the most important is the ability to interrogate our own thinking and perceptions and consider contingencies.

If this, then that.

If not that, then what?

The ability to re-represent your own thinking gives you the scope to learn more efficiently from experience and, crucially, to plan for different eventualities.

It reduces the likelihood of repeating your mistakes. (Although, if you a frustrated golfer, or a golf coach, you might have doubts about this.)

CHAPTER 5: THE ONE, SINGLE CAUSE OF PRESSURE

For the first few hundred thousand years of human existence, survival and reproduction were clear evolutionary priorities. Fulfilling basic needs took up most of our time and energies.

You don't need to be an anthropologist to appreciate how the capacity for self-reflection and to consider contingencies has redefined these priorities and brought us to where we find ourselves today.

Most golfers live in societies where technology has made the environment much safer and more comfortable. Survival is more assured and less physically taxing. Life expectancy has increased. We are so successful in navigating the process of reproduction that ways and means to control and limit our populations are the norm.

Fulfilling basic needs takes less time and effort. Instead of hunting and gathering, dinner gets delivered to the door. Clean water and sanitation are taken for granted.

With more time available for contemplation, our desires have become more sophisticated and refined. Just existing isn't enough. We want a richer, more satisfying, more varied experience of life.

We want to experience a wider range of feelings. To anticipate, to enjoy, to learn, to realise our potentials, to find meaning.

Perhaps this is why we play. Maybe the urge to play games evolved to expand and vary our experiences once the essentials of life had become more assured?

What Do You Really Want?

Whenever the inhabitants of a stable, modern society are asked what they most want in life, the most common answer is:

To be happy.

Even if we don't realise it at the time, most of our activity from moment to moment is in pursuit of this feeling of well-being, peace, freedom, joy, and contentment commonly referred to as 'happiness'.

This feeling is universally known, although we have many different words for it. If I discussed the matter with a Chinese-speaker or someone from an Inuit tribe, they would use different terminology. But they would certainly recognise the feeling.

Where does this innate, deep-rooted intuition that happiness is the purpose of life come from?

Well, when we are in this feeling, we stop wanting, needing, striving, and seeking. We might say that our purpose has been fulfilled. The potentials of life in that moment have been realised.

The pursuit of happiness is what drives us to work to earn money, start relationships, play games, create and build, and want to achieve things. We associate a feeling of happiness with success in all these activities.

(Again, please don't take my word for this. Check it against your own experience. There is a thought experiment at the end of this chapter to assist.)

When not searching for happiness, many people spend considerable time and energy struggling against circumstances or events they suspect may stop them from being happy.

These twin desires, seeking happiness and resisting unhappiness, are the main motivators for a wide range of human activity.

Including the game of golf.

As we indulge in these activities, lurking in the shadows of the mind at a semi-conscious level is the question: *What might this mean for me?*

It takes on many different guises and variations as life unfolds and feelings come and go.

What might this [situation, event, occurrence, change in circumstances] mean for me? How will I feel if...?

A Threat to Survival – of Whom?

Remember that in the past this continuous monitoring and assessment was concerned with survival – for the individual and consequently of the species.

But now in modern, safer times, our wants and needs have diversified. Worries about survival are less immediate than concerns about happiness, well-being, peace, freedom, fulfilment. It could be said that the nature of our desires is evolving to become more spiritual rather than 'physical', as seen from the materialist standpoint previously described.

So, the question *What might this mean for me?* develops into:

Does 'this' mean I'm going to be happy? If so, how can I encourage or prolong it?

Does 'this' mean I'm going to be unhappy? If so, how can I prevent it or overcome it?

This train of thinking is the cause of all the sensations associated with pressure or stress both on and off the golf course.

Our biological systems have not evolved at the same rate as our psychological ones. A negative evaluation of the query *'What might this mean for me?'* still leads to a fight-or-flight response. Heightened arousal, tension in the body. The release of potent stimulants into the limbic system. Feelings of anxiety, insecurity, or fear. The shutting down of all non-essential processes.

This was (and remains) an important survival mechanism in a less benign environment. An asset when it comes to taking down a prey animal, defending your territory, or running for your life. But these powerful bodily sensations are unwanted complications in tasks such as holing a slippery, downhill three-footer for par, or nipping a delicate chip shot off a tightly mown fairway.

A tee shot sailing out of bounds or a short putt missed, events we imagine could deny our future happiness, are classified as a threat to survival.

Psychological peril is confused with an existential one.

The Downside of Metacognition

In the previous chapter, I suggested that there is a price to pay for the obvious evolutionary benefits that self-reflective metacognition has afforded us. (If you are familiar with the Old Testament, this cost is acknowledged in the fable of Adam and Eve.)

Along with the ability to plan, we have the capacity to worry about what the future might have in store for us. As well as reflecting on past events and learning from them, we can have regrets. We can wish things might have happened differently and beat ourselves up for the mistakes made or be embarrassed by our behaviour.

Contemplating contingencies is a useful ability. But with it comes the potential to catastrophise. To sabotage our peace of mind with imaginings of disastrous situations, and to paralyse ourselves through procrastination.

A self-aware intellect is a powerful tool, but is one that needs to be applied with care. It can be a blessing one minute and a curse the next.

Most golfers will be familiar with the more troublesome patterns of thinking that metacognition makes available. How it takes us away from the here and now. All the more reason for a wise golfer to invest some time and energy understanding how the mind really works.

The Game of Golf and the Game of Life

So, let's see how an alternative explanation of our experience leads to a more coherent interpretation of the nature of reality (previously explored in Chapter 4.)

What does the question of whether reality is mental or physical mean for you and your golf?

Belief in a reality that is in essence, material comes with implications. One of which is the (reasonable) assumption that happiness is *dependent on the situation in the physical world*, on circumstances, events, and relationships.

After all, in this paradigm, subjective experience (consciousness, thoughts, feelings, perceptions) *depends upon and arises from* the material substance that your body and brain is composed of.

For happy feelings to arise, an apparently logical

deduction is that the 'physical' world of your environment needs to be arranged in a way that meets your expectations.

Therefore, seeking and resisting are powerful driving forces in activities (such as golf), in dealing with objects (money and possessions), in relationships, and in the states of mind experienced around these activities and objects.

We believe that hitting a good golf shot is the cause of happiness. And that hitting a bad one is the cause of unhappiness.

That a par leads to a better feeling than a bogey.

That winning a championship will bring satisfaction and fulfilment, while missing the cut will cause disappointment and embarrassment.

The patterns that play out in a game of golf seem to be a microcosm of the patterns that play out in the game of life.

We pursue outcomes we think will make us happy. And strive to avoid outcomes we anticipate will prevent happiness.

For anyone who has played golf for more than a few weeks, these outcomes and the feelings that accompany them indeed *seem borne out in our experiences*. The belief that poor golf leads to suffering, while results that match or exceed predictions equals happiness is reinforced.

As a result, we become prisoners of our expectations on the golf course rather than accepting and finding meaning in the challenge of the game. You cannot be frustrated unless you had expectations.

Golf becomes an addiction that persists despite the disappointment it regularly brings. Time and effort spent playing or practicing are regarded as an investment that needs justifying with a reward.

The reward is the possibility of relief from that frustration – a few solid, well flighted shots or a decent round. It dangles like a carrot in front of a hungry donkey.

This golfer is trapped in the same loop as a gambler chasing his losses. The more time that elapses between rewards, the more desperate he becomes.

A Case of Mistaken Identity

So, in short, our mental and physical processes have become confused about what constitutes a threat to well-being.

A system that was beneficial for our biological safety in the earlier stages of evolution has become a liability now that the risk is of a different nature. Imagine an alarm in your house that is impossible to switch off and that cannot distinguish between an intruder and a guest.

I hope this explains why a fully grown adult

might experience panic attack symptoms when faced with the simple and non-essential task of stroking a small, white ball into a hole from a short distance away.

This theory is nothing new in the world of performance coaching. The difference lies in what a logical response to the problem might be.

Most techniques offered by mainstream coaches and psychologists focus on trying to mitigate the *consequences* of this faulty threat assessment.

Positive thinking, visualisation, deep-breathing or relaxation exercises are all useful tools and might work for some people some of the time. But they all just deal with *symptoms*.

These strategies are intended to be applied after feelings of fear and anxiety have arisen. But in difficult moments, you are least likely to be thinking clearly enough to apply them.

We already know that feelings don't arise from situations or circumstances.

Feelings come from your thinking. And attempting to reframe your thinking is just another form of deceiving yourself. It's hard to pretend you don't care about missing a putt when your emotions are screaming that you do.

There is an alternative.

Let's tap our ability to use rationality and reason

to get ahead of the game and make a more accurate assessment of what is really going on. To try to make the alarm system more intelligent and discerning.

Wouldn't it be better to employ the tool of meta-cognition – our highly prized capacity for self-reflection – to cultivate a more harmonious relationship with our thinking rather than pushing it away or trying to fix it?

Rather than focus on the perception of the threat and how to avoid or deal with it, let's try to fully understand the nature of who or what is feeling threatened when faced with a delicate pitch over a bunker to a tight hole location, or a long carry over a water hazard.

To respond to the question *What might this mean for me?* in a skilful manner, you need to make an accurate appraisal of the *situation*. (What is '*this*'?). Are your perceptions and assumptions correct, or are they obscured by your beliefs?

Next you need to assess the possible potential *consequences*. (What might it *mean*?)

But before judgement is made on either, *you need to know who or what the 'me' or the 'I' is that will suffer those consequences*. To whom or what do they apply?

Only then can you start to consider what *anything* really means to you, what value an event, situation, object, or relationship has in your life.

CHAPTER 5: THE ONE, SINGLE CAUSE OF PRESSURE

If you believe that who or what you essentially are is a limited, finite, vulnerable 'physical' entity, then the instinctive response of fight or flight when threatened makes sense.

But what is in danger when you are playing golf?

You know intellectually that a three-footer to win ten quid off a mate isn't a life-or-death situation. So why are your hands shaking? Why have your bowels tightened as though a bear with a grumpy expression has just wandered out of the bushes and towards the putting green?

Something has gone badly wrong in the processing of the *What does this mean to me?* query. An erroneous assumption has been made.

And once that assumption has slipped through, a cascade of further misunderstandings and irrational, illogical decisions and actions follows.

That misjudgement or assumption was made so long ago that you have probably forgotten ever making it. I hope Chapter 4 might have jogged your memory.

In Chapter 6, the final chapter of Part One, we will retrace our steps to establish exactly where the wrong turn was taken and begin to consider how we might get back on track.

Thought Experiment:

Think about the last time you were successful, or

when you attained or achieved something?

What did you do? What did it feel like?

Now try to remember how long the feeling lasted?

What might that tell you about what we are really looking for in life?

Key Points from Chapter 5:
- Self-awareness (conscious metacognition) is the mental attribute that sets us apart from most other sentient beings.
- All psychological stress and anxiety (pressure) can be traced back to a single thought.
- In modern, safer, less-precarious societies, our priorities have evolved from survival and reproduction to happiness and fulfilment.
- Human psychology is evolving faster than our biological systems.
- Metacognition comes with a cost – one that most golfers will be only too familiar with.
- Seeking happiness and resisting unhappiness are key drivers in most human activity – including golf.
- Our fears and anxieties when we play arise from a misunderstanding about who or what is in danger.

CHAPTER 6

Who Are You?

'Only that which is always with you can be said to be your self and if you look simply at experience, only awareness is always with you.'

Rupert Spira

IN THE PREVIOUS CHAPTER, the origins of the feelings of fear and anxiety that afflict many golfers were identified.

In summary, we have forgotten who we really are. We have become primarily identified with our physical form and overlooked our true, essentially spiritual nature. We have come to believe that happiness and fulfilment depend on the material world conforming to allow achievements and attainment.

Consequently, our base-level survival systems respond as if denial of our ambitions were an existential danger by triggering a physical response felt as sensations in the body.

Many psychological techniques recognise this

faulty feedback loop. But rather than address the fundamental issue, a variety of complex and illogical solutions are suggested, ignoring the true cause of the feelings.

If you believe that subjective experience (awareness, thoughts, feelings, perceptions, etc.) arises in the brain and needs to be controlled and manipulated, developing coping strategies to deal with the symptoms seems the only viable option.

A simple question that would allow a suffering golfer to escape the trap is overlooked.

Who or what is under threat here?

Or,

To whom does this matter?

When the ball is heading towards the water hazard and the question *What does this mean for me?* arises, to whom or what does the word *'me'* refer?

If you don't know the truth about who or what you essentially are, how can you even begin to understand what golf, or anything else in your life means?

It Starts Before Golf

When writing *The Three Principles of Outstanding Golf* back in 2016, it seemed to me, (as I'm sure it does for most people), that awareness was personal. Something I was doing. Something that came and went.

Something that could be directed and focused. Lost and found.

Dropping this belief and seeing the truth of awareness was life changing. Challenges that needed overcoming slipped down the to do list. The meanings I had arbitrarily imposed on the game changed. Understanding true nature is the most important lesson I have learned.

With hindsight, all the hours on the range, all the thousands of miles travelled around the world, all the struggles and frustrations were building up to understanding something beyond golf.

In modern language, the experience of knowing, or being aware, is referred to as 'consciousness'. Consciousness is the awareness by which all experience is known.

Ask yourself: *Have I ever experienced anything outside of awareness?*

The answer should be obvious.

But like many things familiar to us, awareness is taken for granted. Consciousness is overlooked in the same way that the screen gets overlooked when you watch golf on television. The screen is always present. But you don't notice it when the coverage starts. It disappears into the background as your attention becomes absorbed by the story playing out in the pictures and audio.

Likewise, we are obsessed by the content of our thoughts, our feelings, sensations, and perceptions. The story of 'me'. Rarely, if ever, do we consider what makes experiencing those thoughts, feelings, sensations, and perceptions possible.

As mentioned in Chapter 5, for centuries, philosophers and scientists have been contemplating the question: *What is the nature of consciousness?*

(For those interested in this enquiry, I suggest following the line of philosophical thought that runs from Plato to Descartes; Bishop Berkeley, Kant, and Schopenhauer; through to modern thinkers such as Carl Jung, Aldous Huxley and Bernardo Kastrup.)

The question contains a paradox. Consciousness itself has no objective qualities. It has no dimensions. It cannot be seen, felt, measured, or described with words. Everyone knows what consciousness does but it isn't possible to say exactly what it is. There is a long tradition of using silence as a teaching method.

Our languages have evolved to describe duality. There are subjects and objects, verbs and nouns. The difficulty in finding words to describe the ultimate context in which all experience – including language – takes place means inevitably that more emphasis is placed on the content of our experience than on the nature of it. It is easy to describe the content of perception. Explaining how a perception came to be is more difficult.

Unsurprisingly, the consequences of this paradox show up in the way we play, learn, and talk about golf. The tangible, material aspects are emphasised over the subtle ones. Far more attention is paid to what the swing should look like, and to relevant measurable parameters such as ball speed, club path, and angle of attack, than to understanding how golfers feel what we feel and why.

Most golfers devote more time and energy to the outer game – the swing, putting stroke, fitness, equipment, etc. – than to learning about the inner game – thinking, feeling, decision-making and what the game means.

If your worldview – the way you understand reality and, therefore, the ultimate context in which the game of golf is played – is founded on a misunderstanding, it shouldn't be a surprise if your reasons for playing become confused and you get in your own way.

The Nature of Experience

In Chapter 3, I suggested that we have two alternatives to guide how we live and relate to the world. We can persist with our beliefs or accept the evidence of our direct experience. Please re-read that chapter if you'd like a reminder of the implications of this choice.

If it seems that truth is more likely found down

the road of experience rather than belief, would it not make sense to better understand the nature of that experience? Rather than clinging on to the belief of a reality based on a yet to be verified substance called 'matter', let's explore the evidence for an alternative. Evidence apparent from our direct experience, qualified and confirmed using logic and reason.

Our human experience has two aspects. That which is perceived and that which perceives. That *which perceives* must be at least as real as *what is perceived*. You can be wrong about the *content* of a perception; such illusions happen regularly. But the *fact* of perceiving is undeniable.

Everything that is perceived or known is known by awareness, or consciousness.

Consciousness is the ultimate constant, the most consistent element of our lives. To be aware of change, there must be *some aspect* that stays the same. The *content* of experience – thoughts, feelings, sensations, and perceptions – is always changing. That which perceives or *knows* experience (awareness) never does.

Every day you play is different. No round of golf is identical. Every shot is different. No swing feels exactly the same. Hole locations change, tee positions change, weather conditions change. But the *awareness* of all those elements has never changed.

It is always, and has always been, the same.

So, whatever is known, whatever you accept as 'reality', is only understood in the terms of your understanding of consciousness. If you wear tinted sunglasses on the golf course, the colours you see through them will not truly represent those of the grass, the trees, the sky. It will be a distortion of what is really out there.

If you don't understand the *nature* of awareness by which your life is known, can you really understand the *content* of your life experience? Your understanding will be partial, or distorted.

If you don't recognise the awareness by which you know your 'self', do you really know who you are?

Consciousness is the context within which experience is created for us via thought and perception. This creative process can only happen within awareness, within consciousness. If it happened outside of awareness, *you wouldn't know about it.* There wouldn't *be* an experience.

On the blank screen of awareness, thought creates a perception of the world informed by the data captured by the senses. You don't see *with* your eyes; you see *through* them.

Even when you are sleeping, consciousness is present. Sleep is not the absence of awareness. It is the awareness of absence. How could you be disturbed by an external noise or a dream if awareness wasn't aware?

Consciousness is eternal, unchanging. It is the most fundamental, the most basic element of the human experience. It is the arena in which your experience of life unfolds.

You Are Consciousness

The easiest mistake to make as a human being is to forget who you really are. This forgetting is precipitated, encouraged, and reinforced by cultural attachment to the materialist paradigm.

Getting in your own way is simply forgetting that your true nature, your essence – that aspect of you which doesn't change, which doesn't come or go – is awareness, or consciousness.

'You' isn't something physical or material. The physical, the material, is *known by* awareness. It is secondary. It changes with time. It comes and it goes.

Most people believe themselves to be a body inhabited by a mind. They believe that consciousness somehow emanates from this entity. But the moment you start to examine this assumption more closely, the absurdity of this belief becomes apparent.

Do you say: 'I have a body' or 'I am a body'?

'I have a mind' or 'I am a mind'?

Your physical form has changed significantly throughout your life. Cells are constantly dying and

CHAPTER 6: WHO ARE YOU?

being replaced. The body you swing a golf club with now is not the body you experienced five or ten years ago. Yet your deepest intuition about who you are is the same as it was when you were a small child.

You still refer to yourself as 'me' or 'I' despite the components of your biological structures having been regenerated many times over.

If you were to lose part of your anatomy, you would still refer to yourself as 'I' or 'me'. You don't feel any less 'you' if you go on a diet or have a haircut. Your body is more akin to the house you inhabit or the vehicle you drive than it is your essential being.

Likewise, your inner being, your mind. Your thoughts, feelings, preferences, likes, dislikes, beliefs, behaviours, and relationships have varied, come, and gone in one way or another since you were a child. Yet you still feel your 'self' as the same awareness of them – and refer to it as such.

You have referred to yourself as 'I' from the moment you could speak.

To what then, does the word *'my'* refer to in the previous phrases? To what do we deeply intuit the mind and body belong?

It is to the awareness of them.

The 'me' or 'I' referred to in our thoughts and actions from moment to moment is awareness, or consciousness.

That is who you really are.

This recognition allows us to proceed with the train of reasoning started in the previous chapter. When most people ask, *'What does this mean for me?'* they have innocently made a wrong assumption about who or what the 'me' they are referring to actually is.

If your attachment is to the 'you' that is the central character in the story of your life – a limited, finite body/mind – it's natural for you to worry about the destiny of that body/mind. You will be concerned whether the story has a happy ending.

But who or what knows your story? From whose perspective is the story being told? To whom does the story belong?

Golf is probably a big part of your life. If you have invested time, effort, and money into 'becoming' someone or achieving something in the game, when the story seems to be heading in an undesirable direction, your feelings will certainly warn you of impending danger.

This experience is the stress and pressure well known by golfers. But it isn't caused by situation or circumstance.

It arises from a case of mistaken identity.

There Is Only One Reality

In Chapter 4, we questioned the common belief that there are two separate realities: the 'reality' of our inner lives – thoughts, feelings, perceptions, and sensations known via awareness – and the apparent external 'reality' of the physical world.

'Mind' and 'matter' as they are commonly described.

But our only experience of the matter from which we are told the universe is created is our knowing of it. This knowing happens in awareness. This would seem to confirm the deeply held intuition that there is only one reality.

And it is spiritual, not physical or material.

In the language of philosophical idealism, (in contrast to materialism) awareness, or consciousness, is the *ontological primitive*.

Every theory about the nature of reality needs to have something at the bottom of the reduction base. This is the ground level. The baseline. That from which everything else is derived and can be explained but itself cannot be explained in terms of something else.

It just is what it is.

For materialism, the bottom of the reduction base is the field of subatomic particles described in the Standard Model (mentioned in Chapter 4.)

Yet this model and the objects and structures within it cannot account for or explain consciousness – subjective experience. Yet we know beyond any doubt that reality perceives.

All objects and structures are known *by* awareness.

How can the bottom of the reduction base, the primary element by which everything else can be explained, have something that stands outside it?

It doesn't make sense.

Not only does our intuition suggest that there is only one reality, and it is non-material in nature, but logic and reason point to the same conclusion!

Most human beings would agree that when head and heart are in alignment we are probably getting close to the truth.

The One Eye of the World

So, what other evidence can we gather from direct experience to confirm our intuitions about the unitary nature of reality?

Well, no matter how hard I try, I cannot find an edge or outer limit to awareness. I can't remember a beginning to it. And I can't find a point where it ends. It seems not to be limited by either time or space.

As with matter, time and space seem to be conceptual frameworks that appear *within* awareness.

I have discussed this matter with other curious people over the last few years. And guess what? Their intuition is telling them the same thing. Their experience of awareness finds the same limitless, infinite qualities.

Test it for yourself. See if you can find a boundary to awareness? The point where it starts or where it ends. Does it have edges, a bottom, or a top?

If my sense of awareness has no limits, and neither does that of other people, what does this suggest? The evidence infers that rather than being eight billion individual awarenesses, there is one awareness, experiencing from eight billion individual perspectives or viewpoints.

'The one eye of the world, which looks out from all knowing creatures', as German philosopher Arthur Schopenhauer wrote more than 200 years ago.

Consciousness is the reality that perceives. Consciousness is not dependent on the mind. It is unlimited, not dependent on anything. This has profound implications.

Ask yourself, what would you prefer: to be a body without consciousness, or to be consciousness without a body?

If it is the latter, two facts become clear. The first is that what you really identify with is not your physical form, it is awareness. If so, what you mean by death, is not the end of the body, it is the end of awareness.

Realising your true nature allows a reassessment of your relationship with fear. You can acknowledge there is no evidence that consciousness shares the limitations of the body or the mind. The fear of death, the fear of absolute disappearance releases its grip.

When you recognise that your biggest fear was an illusion, a two-footer on the 18th green to win the big match can be seen in a new light.

Consciousness has a reality of its own. The awareness that is perceiving these words right now is real. You aren't making it up.

The words themselves could be made up. This could be a dream that you are reading a book. But, regardless, the awareness by which you are aware of the dream is the same. It cannot be denied. Our intuition that consciousness is real has deep foundations.

We have another strong intuition – that this reality is singular.

This reality perceives.

And what you refer to as 'I' or 'me' is it.

Another Thought Experiment

Ask yourself the simple question: *Am I aware?*

This is perhaps the easiest, most direct way to begin a journey of self-enquiry.

The answer to the question *Am I aware?* ...

... can only be 'Yes'.

After hearing the question, notice there is a space between the thought that is the enquiry and the thought that is the answer.

What happens in-between these two thoughts is not an activity of the mind, because in that moment there is no conception of time or space.

Thinking stops.

There is just a *knowing* from which the answer arises.

To answer the question *Am I aware?* you must *know* the experience of being aware. It isn't a belief or a learned theory.

You must be aware of being aware. If you were not able to know awareness as awareness, how could you answer positively?

At this point, the question becomes *Who or what is the 'I' that is aware of being aware?*

As previously acknowledged, only awareness can be aware. Therefore, in that gap between the question and answer, something significant has occurred.

Awareness has become aware of itself. You have understood who you really are.

(To be precise with language, awareness doesn't *become* aware of itself; awareness is always aware of itself.)

When awareness becomes involved with the creation of a thought, an object, or an activity it merges with it.

For example, when a golf shot is created, awareness is an integral, essential part of that creative process. It becomes absorbed into its creation.

Being aware of being aware – or consciousness knowing itself – is realised in-between two activities of the mind, be they thoughts or perceptions, feelings, or sensations.

In the hesitation between the question *Am I aware?* and the response, the mind ceases its activity and, as a result, is freed from its limitations and thereby knows itself as it truly is.

Awareness resumes awareness of awareness.

This revelation, awareness turning inwards to face itself, is highly significant for anyone who struggles with a stream of troubling thoughts, memories, and imaginings.

To understand that your experience is simply

composed of thoughts, feelings, sensations, and perceptions arising in consciousness is to realise that *you are not your thoughts.*

The idea that feelings aren't caused by your circumstances becomes a reality. They are not the result of the shot you just hit, the numbers on your scorecard, the people watching from the clubhouse terrace, or the outcome of a match.

Feelings arise from the experience being created in the moment via thought and consciousness, from identification with one of those thoughts as 'me' or 'I'.

If it weren't for the capacity to be aware of how this happens, then we could never be released from the illusion of the separate self.

Thanks to metacognition, you become aware of being aware. You are at last out of your own way. You are free.

Without the capacity for self-reflection, you could not escape the misunderstanding that you are your thoughts, your feelings, perceptions, and sensations.

Someone who believes everything they think is reality – is insane.

Feelings of isolation and insecurity, a low or anxious mood, are no longer maintained once you remember how consciousness and thought are working in seamless harmony to create your experience of life.

The One Thing You Need to Know

Your capacity to go beyond personal thought, to realise where your thinking is coming from, is constantly available to you. The more you look to the *nature* of experience rather than trying to control the *content* of experience, the less challenging and more straightforward golf and life seem to become.

In fact, for your state of mind to be radically different, you don't need to convince yourself of what I am suggesting here. Simply questioning the long-standing belief that you are something physical, something limited, something finite and constrained is enough for life-changing insights to occur.

Pause for a moment to consider the implications of this revelation. How might life and golf be different if you stopped trying to become something more or better?

If you could just relax into the knowing that you are perfect, well, and whole exactly as you are, right here right now?

If you saw that all the problems and challenges, all the stresses and pressures you were experiencing were just due to conditions innocently placed on your own happiness. Beliefs picked up from the culture you have been immersed in from birth.

How might you live and play the game from this new understanding?

In Part Two of the book, we will explore how

creativity, confidence, concentration, consistency, and composure – five of the mental characteristics golfers desire most – can be enjoyed simply through a deeper understanding of how your experience of life is realised.

We will see how realising just one thing – the nature of awareness, or consciousness – is the secret to getting out of your own way and allowing your potential as a golfer to shine through.

Key Points from Chapter 6:
- Describing awareness, or consciousness is impossible. This means that the most fundamental aspect of experience is commonly overlooked.
- The ultimate context of your life is awareness, or consciousness. Without consciousness, you would not have experience.
- Consciousness is constant and unchanging.
- Consciousness is who you essentially are, not something you do. You are not the central character in the story of 'you'. You are *what knows or is aware* of the story.
- Consciousness is the only reality. The reality that perceives. This awareness is the referent when you say the word 'me' or 'I'.
- Becoming aware of being aware is the easiest, simplest, and most natural realisation. It is the most powerful thing you can do to get out of your own way.

Summing Up Part One
A New Understanding

Chapter 6 completes the first part of the book. Before we go on to consider the implications of this new understanding for your golf, let's once again review the train of reasoning we have followed thus far.

We have identified the common misunderstandings that might lead to a golfer innocently sabotaging their own performance and enjoyment. Getting in their own way, in the common parlance.

In Chapter 1, the Introduction, the first clue in the puzzle was noted. We acknowledge the internal conversations that many golfers experience when they play.

Would understanding the *nature* of that narrative – investigating who appears to be talking to whom and why – allow a more satisfying experience of the game? Rather than following the usual approach of analysing and trying to fix the *content* of that dialogue?

In Chapter 2, we explore the intuition of many golfers that insight – learning and understanding something new – is a logical step to playing the game more proficiently. The multimillion-dollar golf instruction industry is fuelled by this belief.

But as many have discovered, just gathering more knowledge about golf doesn't necessarily make you a more skilful golfer. Or make for a more enjoyable game.

Rather than constantly breaking apart and trying to rebuild your technique, perhaps understanding who is playing, the entity who is trying to learn, might be a more productive line of enquiry and lead to better, more satisfying golf.

Chapter 3 identifies a common mistake many golfers make when trying to improve. Instead of trusting our own direct experience of reality, we innocently follow beliefs acquired from the prevailing culture and from other golfers.

Despite struggling, we fail to interrogate those beliefs. We cling to them in the face of mounting evidence that they might be the cause of the problems.

The most durable belief subscribed to is the story about who a person thinks they are. As we have seen, this case of mistaken identity causes both internal and external conflict – on and off the golf course.

In Chapter 4, it is suggested that this questionable belief is grounded in another – that the true nature of reality is material or physical. Could this outdated and unproven assumption be the hidden axiom blinding golfers to their essential identity and limiting their potential?

In Chapter 5, the one single thought that is the cause of pressure and stress in golf and in other areas of life is acknowledged. The consequences of attachment to the unfounded beliefs identified in the previous chapters become clear. If you believe you are something that you are not, the true meaning of activities, achievements, and relationships will be elusive.

The double-edged sword of metacognition is the cause of psychological suffering. But it is also the tool that can set us free.

Chapter 6 is the most important in the whole book. The critical question posed in Chapter 5 – *Who are you?* – is explored in detail. Acknowledging resistance to the possibility that your true nature is consciousness, or awareness (the two words are used synonymously), is the first step to getting out of your own way.

Without consciousness, there is no experience. It is constant and unchanging. The ultimate context of your life is consciousness. Your 'life', in the everyday usage of the word, is a flow of experiences connected by and observed from a single aspect of awareness.

Consciousness is who you essentially are; not

something you do. You are not the central character in the story of 'You'. You are what knows or is aware of the story.

Consciousness is the only reality. The reality that perceives. This awareness is the referent when you say the words *me* or *I*. Questioning the belief that you are a limited, finite body/mind is the key to getting out of your own way and realising your potential as a golfer.

What to do Next

The first part of the book is most important. I hope I have explained the problems with the current mainstream view – and made a persuasive argument for consideration of an alternative.

In the next part, we will explore the implications of this new perspective in terms of the mental attributes most valued and sought by golfers. There is no need to read each chapter in turn. Feel free to skip to the topic you are most curious about.

You can come back to read the others at any time. If at some point you seem to be having difficulty with a particular part of the mental side of the game, I suggest you re-read the first six chapters of the book, and then move on to the one that specifically addresses that aspect.

As I mentioned in the introduction, there is only one thing you need to understand. But the implications will vary from person to person and situation to situation. From my own perspective, this is the fun part. Both for myself, and for the golfers I work with.

Every day, every round, is an opportunity to see how life unfolds in the light of a fresh, new way of understanding reality.

PART TWO
Implications

CHAPTER 7

The Truth About Confidence

'You have put much energy into building a prison for yourself. Now spend as much on demolishing it. In fact, demolition is easy. For the false dissolves when it is discovered.'

Nisargadatta

WHEN A GOLFER STARTS LOOKING FOR HELP with their game, confidence is the mental trait or attribute most feel they are lacking. This comes from the widely held belief that having confidence produces better golf, while self-doubt can lead to playing badly. Searching for or trying to build confidence is a common sign of a golfer getting in their own way. And it is completely unnecessary.

In Chapter 3, we observed that beliefs are often held in conflict with our direct experience. The belief that you need to feel confident to play well is a myth that is dispelled with a moment of closer examination.

Can you remember a time when you had some

doubts about your form or abilities but played well? And then see if you can recall an occasion when you felt good standing over a shot but messed it up.

If you can recall just a single example of either, then you might want to re-evaluate your beliefs about the effects of confidence.

The theory that there is a causal relationship between confidence and performance does not stand up under scrutiny. It is disproved in the light of direct experience.

In this chapter, we will look at why the feeling of confidence is coveted and why belief in its powers is actually what distracts golfers who want to play their best golf more often.

Are You Aware?

In Chapter 6, we explored some intuitions about the nature of consciousness, or awareness (in this context, the two words are interchangeable).

Here is a brief reminder.

Consciousness is the awareness by which all experience is known (feelings of confidence, or self-doubt are one such experience.)

You have never experienced anything outside of awareness. Feel free to test this assertion using your logical and rational thinking mind. If something were to happen outside awareness, how could you experience it? How would it be an experience?

It's instructive that when many people are asked the question *Are you aware?* they reply, 'Aware of what?'

There is no recognition of a separation between awareness and the experience of which they are aware.

You are not your thoughts. Seeing the difference between experience and the *knowing of* that experience is an important first step. The separation between thought and that by which thought is known seems a revelation.

But soon after this realisation, there is nothing more normal, more familiar, or better known than the experience of being aware.

Who Is 'In the Way?'

There are other ways of asking the question posed in Chapter 1:

When the expression 'getting out of your own way' is used, who is in the way of whom? In the context of this chapter, who is stopping whom from feeling confident?

Once you notice that you are aware and recognise awareness as the most direct and immediate experience available, you might ask yourself:

What is it that knows I am aware?

Or, *what is it that knows the experience of knowing?*

In other words, who or what is really getting in the way, the knowing or that which is known? Let's find out.

The customary name for the experience of being aware, or knowing, is 'I'.

'I' am aware of the flag on the green.

'I' am aware of the water on the right of the fairway.

'I' am aware that my playing partner is talking on my backswing.

'I' am aware that a par on the 18th means my handicap will come down.

'I' am aware that I'm leading the tournament.

'I' am aware of some anxious feelings.

'I' am feeling confident.

The experience, *'I am'* is awareness's experience of itself.

Therefore, your knowledge of your true 'self' is awareness's knowledge of *itself*.

If you have never investigated the nature of awareness as we are doing here, or through another spiritual practice, you are probably living in a misunderstanding about who or what you essentially are.

This is why the concept of 'getting out of your

CHAPTER 7: THE TRUTH ABOUT CONFIDENCE

own way' is confusing for so many golfers.

You imagine yourself a separate entity. This entity is a collection of thoughts, feelings, images, memories, sensations, and perceptions. It lives in what you think of as 'your body', controlled by 'your mind'. This is commonly referred to as your ego.

You forget your true self – pure awareness – taking something that is an activity of this mind, which is a derivative of your brain, *as you*. You believe yourself to be the main character in the story about who you think you are.

The veiling, or forgetting of awareness, its refraction into a separate self, or ego means that the inherent peace and security of knowing your own being is no longer felt.

Peace and happiness are obscured by feelings of insecurity, self-doubt, and a lack of confidence.

You are getting in your own way.

Any time you feel like this, or you long for confidence, it's a sign you have turned away from awareness. You have bought into the story your thinking is telling about who you *believe* yourself to be.

The forgetting of your true nature is the cause of all psychological suffering. The realisation, or remembering, of true nature as we look within is the source of the security and confidence we know and enjoy.

'I' Am Not My Body

Consciousness can be imagined as the screen onto which our thoughts, perceptions, and sensations are projected, allowing us to be aware of them.

When these ideas, beliefs, and concepts relate to the mind and the body to which it seems 'I' is attached, the oldest illusion known to humankind comes in to play. The belief that you are a finite separate self, or ego. (This is the 'fall from grace' referred to in the Old Testament and other scriptures.)

Recognising the difference between who you truly are, and the illusion of this separate self leads to a transformation of your experience.

Fresh implications about what you thought of as 'confidence' may become apparent when you become aware of being aware.

Only the separate self feels it needs to be confident.

Only the separate self can believe itself lacking confidence.

Only the body/mind perception is limited, finite, vulnerable, and inadequate.

Awareness is none of these things.

Our concept of confidence mirrors the misunderstanding many people have about happiness, as discussed in Chapter 5. They believe it is something they either have or haven't got. Something they can lose and regain. Something that needs to be built up or acquired through achievements or attainment.

When the nature of your true self is understood, you realise that happiness is simply the knowing of your own being as it is. It is always there. It just sometimes gets forgotten and covered up by insecure thinking, by self-doubt.

The same is true of confidence. Indeed, confidence could be added to the list of words that describe the knowing of well-being, joy, peace and contentment. The freedom enjoyed in the absence of seeking or resisting.

True confidence is the unshakeable knowing 'I will be OK no matter what happens'. What happens is experience. Awareness is what knows experience.

Confidence and the Present Moment

When you look for confidence in memories of the last good round you played, or what your coach said about your golf swing, or the number of three-footers in a row you have holed on the practice putting green; or when you look for reasons why you might feel anxious or insecure, you are reinforcing an illusion.

The first mistake is that *there is something or someone* that can feel confident or not confident. And second, that those feelings are coming from a situation or circumstance independent and separate from you.

Neither of which are true.

In attempting to project awareness more strongly towards objective experience, in searching for reasons why you are not feeling confident, the separate self is reinforced and disconnection from its source is felt more intensely.

When you turn your attention in the opposite direction, towards who you truly are, awareness relaxes back into itself. Feelings of happiness, peace, calmness, and confidence with which we are familiar are allowed to return.

There is no longer attachment to outcome or results. You are living in the present moment. In the now, there is only confidence. Doubt and insecurity only exist in thoughts about past or future. A linear concept of time is another belief that doesn't hold up considering what current experience (and recent experiments in foundations of physics) tells us.

Human beings can only know the now.

A bad memory, a thought about a past event that didn't meet your expectations and caused suffering (mental 'scar tissue' as it is sometimes called), is experienced and felt *now* as a lack of confidence.

A worry, an imagining about a future that might

not turn out as hoped, is experienced and felt *now* as anxiety or self-doubt.

When did now start? When will now end?

The concept of life as a timeline is just that. A concept. It does not fit with the way actual experience is perceived or felt.

It is a useful concept for booking a lesson or tee reservation, or for arranging a golf trip, but in the present moment time itself is never experienced. It is *always* now.

Everything you believe to be you will be destroyed by time. Your thoughts, your feelings, your story. Even your body and mind. But time cannot destroy the present moment.

Awareness destroys time. Only the present moment is real.

The present moment is where confidence lives. And where your golf is played.

Dealing With a Loss of Form

There might come a moment when your enthusiasm for golf runs out.

You are at your lowest ebb. Questions whether it is all worth it arise. The clubs are confined to the darkest corner of the garage, and you decide to take a break from the game.

Typically, at this point all known remedies will have failed. Multiple lessons from different instructors. A fortune spent on new equipment, books read, instruction videos watched. All possibilities in the world of form have been explored and discarded.

Confidence is a distant memory.

This can sometimes be the moment when the separate self falls away allowing an insight to occur. There is nowhere left to turn but within. You give up. Surrender. Thought subsides. You come back to the present. You inadvertently get out of your own way.

Suddenly, a glimpse of what has always been there, but you were too busy looking outside to notice it. You realise that, actually, right here, right now, it's OK. The seeking and resisting stops with that thought.

This brief encounter with reality offers a small sense of the freedom that had been missing. After a couple of weeks, the urge to play returns. You retrieve the clubs, go for a few holes on your own. No expectations. The swing feels effortless and easy. Your game improves for a while.

All that the separate self needs to do to recognise its true nature, and therefore rediscover its inherent happiness and confidence, is to understand *what it is not*.

The true self is neither defined or limited by objective experience, by what it does, how it feels or by what happens to it. By what score you just shot, or your handicap, or what other people think of you and your golf.

In the materialist paradigm, this is the opposite of how confidence is defined.

In the mainstream model of reality, the activity of winning or being successful brings confidence, and confidence brings winning and success.

Again, this belief folds under scrutiny based in experience. If it were true, winners would keep winning, and nobody would ever come back from a loss or bad performance.

The feeling of true confidence lies in the knowledge that who you are is OK no matter what. When you become aware of being aware, you understand what this means. Everything material can be lost, but you'll still be you.

You can never lose awareness.

Only an illusory finite mind and body will experience a sense of limitation, lack, jeopardy, fear, or self-doubt. When thoughts of separation and isolation dominate, confidence vanishes.

There is no peace to be found through seeking and resisting. Seeking and resisting are symptoms of forgetting.

In ignorance, you look outside for ways to make yourself feel better, to assuage the doubts and insecurities. Hard work in the gym, grinding on the range, or changing swing technique are familiar coping strategies for many golfers.

Many people spend their whole lives trying and struggling to become 'someone'. Something more, something better. The most freeing, liberating realisation is that you are no one, no 'thing'.

Does what is aware of your personal story have a story?

Unfortunately, attempts to boost confidence by doing, by trying to become, reinforce the illusion of the separate self.

And even if successful in the short term, they ultimately have the opposite effect.

Confidence Is Remembered

You do not need to eradicate the ego – the separate self – to know your true self, to feel confident. The ego is a useful tool with a job to do. It makes sure you have a roof over your head and food on the table.

Trying to escape from your ego is just another form of seeking or resisting. A trap into which thousands of spiritual aspirants fall.

You can never really get out of your own way. How do you take a step away from yourself? How do you avoid something that doesn't exist?

You were never in your own way to begin with!

There is no ego to be eliminated. Attempts to do so simply lends credence and prolongs the illusion of its existence. Trying to destroy or avoid the separate self is to maintain the separate self. The ego constantly looks for ways to reinvent and reassert control. The quest to 'become a more-enlightened being' is a classic trick of the mind.

'Who you think you are' is a fabrication that only seems to exist from its own illusory point of view. All experiences and illusions, however, have a reality to them. An illusion is not non-existent. It is an experience that is not as it appears to be.

The actual reality of the separate self or finite mind is infinite awareness, consciousness. This returning of awareness to itself – becoming aware of being aware – is the essence of prayer and meditation.

It is sometimes referred to as the 'direct path' to peace, happiness, and fulfilment. But it isn't really a path. There is no journey to take.

There is no route from you to you.

To become aware of awareness, you do not need to go to church, sit on a mat, walk in nature, or repeat a mantra. The experience is available to all, always.

As you realise true nature, golf becomes a meditation. It becomes an expression of who you truly are.

Golf played from knowing is as much an expression of consciousness as a monk sitting in prayer.

There is nowhere to get to, no one to become. No outcome or result can make you more alive, more worthy, or more fulfilled than you are at this present moment.

That is all confidence really is.

It is the remembering of who you really are.

Key Points from Chapter 7:
- Confidence is perhaps the most overrated mental trait.
- The customary name given to the experience of being aware is 'I'. 'I lack confidence' is an abbreviation of 'I am aware I don't feel confident.'
- Only the ego, or separate self, can claim a lack of confidence. Think carefully for a moment about the expression 'self-doubt', often used as an antonym of confidence.
- In the present moment, there is only confidence. Doubts only exist in relation to the past or the future, neither of which have ever been experienced.
- True confidence is the embodied understanding that you are OK no matter what happens.
- There is no requirement to manage, confront, or eliminate the ego. In understanding its true nature, you can understand your own.

CHAPTER 8

The Source of Creativity

'Imagination is receiving mode.'

Abraham Hicks

Many golfers are confused when it comes to creativity in their game. On the one hand, we have been led to believe that golfing success (and therefore happiness) will come from repetition, from the known, from meeting expectations, from orthodoxy, from control.

On the other hand, we love golfers who are creative, innovative, mercurial, and inspired. We enjoy the challenge of playing a recovery shot from the trees. Spotting a gap in the branches, imagining the strike that will send the shot curving in the air, then bouncing and scuttling up onto the front edge of the green.

If you were really in control, how would such opportunities arise?

Some of the most memorable shots seemed impossible yet somehow came into being. Holing for a birdie from a buried lie in the face of a deep greenside bunker. The match-winning 60 foot putt, up a tiered green with a triple break that finished on the edge of the hole for a gimme.

We prize creativity highly. Yet this isn't reflected in our play, and especially our practice. Hitting ball after ball to the same place, with the same club, in the same way, satisfied if the shot matches our previous effort.

Many golfers prepare in ways that discourage creativity and spontaneity rather than developing those qualities. Preparation that bears little relevance to the way the game is played on the course.

Confusion about the true nature and source of creativity has its roots in the misunderstanding laid out in previous chapters – belief in the material nature of reality and the science used to model it and build technologies.

If you believe that the material is primary and is the ultimate source of manifestation, then emphasising the mechanical, the quantifiable, and being less tolerant of the unpredictable nature of thought and feeling makes sense. Golfers attempt to minimise the apparent effects of the inconsistencies and vagaries of the mind. They believe becoming a 'golfing machine' will bring success and therefore happiness.

But before attempting to harness or control the patterns and regularities observed in nature, perhaps it would help to understand the creation of them first.

Can 'Non-Doing' Be Creative?

Awareness is, by its own nature, aware. How could it be anything else?

The separate self, the ego, the central character in the story of who you think you are, is *an activity of awareness, a creation of awareness*.

Therefore, to know awareness is *not* an activity.

Getting out of your own way is not active. It is a non-doing – a cessation. It happens when you stop impeding and interrupting the flow of reality.

Our culture celebrates and rewards doing. Striving, action, making things happen. Taking the credit or apportioning blame then follows. When your ball ends up in the water hazard or finds the bottom of the cup, it sure seems like someone made it go there.

If you turned up for a golf lesson and your instructor didn't advise doing (or not doing) you would be confused. Instruction articles are a staple of most golf magazines. After watching the latest video from your favourite social media golf guru, you want to do the drills, make the changes, apply the techniques he or she is suggesting.

Our cultural attachment to action and reaction is deep rooted. Non-doing is not easy. As many people discovered during the Covid-19 pandemic lockdowns, enforced idleness is challenging. Human nature is dynamic, creative, energetic, enthusiastic. We want to be busy. We like to do. Perhaps the label human beings, is less appropriate than human 'doings'?

And wider culture, of course, permeates the way we approach golf. Non-doing might be an interesting theory. But that 300 yard drive isn't going to hit itself. Who else is going to create it if 'I' don't?

Can you see the trick of the mind inherent in that question? With the 'I thought', a separate 'creator' has been smuggled into the process. As if the creator were somehow distinct from the creation. And that's how it seems if you don't understand how manifestation occurs.

The inspiration to create a golf shot arises as a thought in awareness. And with the following thought, a separate creator (a golfer who hits the shot) also arises. The deception occurs as this 'I thought' assumes responsibility for the previous creative intention.

But when the original impulse arose, no separate creator existed. There was only creation unfolding as a potential of consciousness. The golfer appeared one thought later.

This is our experience from the moment we are born. The 'someone' who is 'doing' is an after-

CHAPTER 8: THE SOURCE OF CREATIVITY

thought, arising in the same way as the intention.

The will to create seems to be within us all, expressed from an early age. You only need to watch young children playing to see the strength of this will. They create from whatever is available in the environment. Whether it is rudimentary art, music, or a game. If opportunity arises, creation unfolds.

Also noticeable is the absence of significant stress, or pressure, or attachment to this creation. A young golfer immersed in the process of creating a golf shot rarely seems deterred by failure to hit the target or do the 'right swing'. There might be a fleeting moment of frustration. But another attempt follows and slowly improvement happens.

A different kind of knowing, of understanding, is present and underpins the process of skill acquisition.

Primary Knowledge

Awareness's knowledge of itself is not a new or special kind of knowledge, yet it is the knowledge on which all other knowledge is based. It is the window through which all experience is viewed, including the experience of creation.

It is a class of knowledge that transcends and underpins all other knowledge and experience. It remains unchanged at all times. It is the only certainty. All other knowledge borrows any relative certainty from it.

Nothing can be known without awareness, yet it is overlooked in favour of our experience of creating objects and events. This experience of an object implies a subject. This subject (creator) comes with the label 'I' or 'me'.

'I' did this or that.

This is how 'I' did it.

That is why 'I' did it.

This happened to 'me'.

When we try to say *how* something should be, or explain *why* something is the way it is, a belief is being shared. We are innocently limiting the limitless and obstructing our innate creativity.

Sometimes after a great golf shot, the realisation occurs that I don't really know how it happened. I was standing behind the ball when an image or feeling arose, an intention to create that beautiful shot. My body arranged itself in a way that felt comfortable and the swing began.

It just unfolded as I observed and felt it happening. The intuition was more that the shot came through me rather than of having 'produced' it.

(As the ball landed by the flag, the ego claimed the credit for 'visualising' the shot and making it happen. As if a thought could be responsible for

CHAPTER 8: THE SOURCE OF CREATIVITY

creating another thought.)

We have already explored the nature of thought and come to see that control or agency over what thought arises in awareness or when it does so is an illusion. How then, could a separate-self take the credit, or indeed the blame, for the creation of a golf swing and the subsequent outcome of the shot?

The intention arises as a thought. Where did that thought come from? Who chose it?

You Cannot Choose to Be Inspired

It would be lovely if I could just sit down with my laptop and say, 'Right, here we go, time for inspiration to strike!' But you can't choose to be inspired. Nor can you choose to be creative. What you can do is get out of the way by acknowledging and embracing the unknown, allowing inspiration and creativity to emerge.

Many golfers will be familiar with the experience of arriving at the course with no expectations. Maybe you hadn't played for a while. Or last time didn't go so well. Or you were rushing to make a tee time after a busy morning.

You weren't thinking about what to do to or how to do it. Your mind was preoccupied with other matters. You rolled onto the first tee, plucked a ball from your bag, took aim down the fairway, and let the shot go. Out of nowhere, your best round of the season emerged.

Sometimes you hear tour players acknowledge their confusion after playing an outstanding round or winning a tournament after a run of poor form. They are at a loss to explain how or why what just happened unfolded as it did.

Then, perhaps after some prompting by an interviewer or well-meaning coach, the intellect is provoked. It starts seeking reasons *why*, in the hope of a repeat performance. To try to ensure that the recipe is captured and can be recreated.

Of course, this is impossible. The magic wasn't in the doing or in the knowledge (from the point of view of the ego) of what happened. The magic was in the dissolution of the separate self, in letting go. In the absence of the 'I thought' freedom is regained. Imagine a great painter being asked to describe each brush stroke in creating a fine work of art then trying to reproduce a facsimile in the same way a few days later.

A memory isn't created at the time of an event. It too arises from awareness later. This is why recollections seem to change over time.

Our essential being, true awareness, is not remembered in the way that an event, an object, or a person can be recalled. Only something with defined, objective qualities can be created and recreated by the mind.

You might remember what you *think* happened, but never how it really happened.

Only a Subject Can Know an Object

That creation occurs is hard to deny. The universe demonstrates its potentials – it is dynamic, creative, energetic. It seems to be going somewhere. Stuff appears and disappears. Things are happening.

So, it shouldn't come as a surprise that human nature, itself a creation of and a fundamental part of that same universe, arising from the same essence, shows similar potentials and tendencies.

Let's remind ourselves of a couple of things we know.

Consciousness is primary. It was here first. Everything in experience – thoughts, feelings, perceptions, and sensations – arises from and in awareness. In that sense, the nature of awareness is creative.

In contrast to materialism, or physicalism, philosophical idealism posits awareness or consciousness as the ontological primitive. It is the bottom of the reduction base. It is the aspect of reality from which everything else is derived and can be explained, but it cannot be explained in terms of something else.

As such, awareness is the source of all creation.

Where did the game of golf begin? History suggests that a few hundred years ago, a thought arose within the awareness of a Scottish shepherd. The inspiration to swipe at a pebble with his crook became an intention and then an action. It happened again and was emulated by others. The game we know as golf was born.

Only awareness can know awareness, and only a subject can know an object. Therefore, to show up, create in, and experience life in 'the world', consciousness creates and assumes the form of the finite mind, or separate self.

It assumes the form of a Scottish shepherd.

Or it assumes the form of what you think of as 'you', the golfer.

There appears to be a creation ... and a 'someone' who created it.

There appears to be a game ... and a 'someone' playing it.

There appears to be a challenge to overcome ... and 'someone' to overcome it.

There appears to be a something 'getting in the way' ... and a 'someone' who's way it is in.

This refraction, this fragmentation of universal consciousness creates and experiences thoughts, feelings, images, objects, and activities. It creates the experience of the golf course, the feeling of the swing. Powerful soaring drives, crisp iron shots, deft chip shots, and accurate putts come into being.

As it does so, its ability to know itself as it is, is lost. In the form of 'you, the golfer', it cannot know pure awareness.

You Are What You Seek

Just as a television programme could be described as the activity of the screen, or a wave could be said to be the activity of the ocean, the finite mind or separate self – the golfer – is an activity of universal consciousness.

A separate self who is seeking awareness – a golfer attempting to escape unhappiness by playing better, deliberately trying to focus or concentrate, to develop a particular mindset, or to get out of their own way – is like an ocean wave seeking water.

It is that which it is looking for.

The ego, or finite mind, is the activity or creativity of awareness in which awareness itself has become merged and enmeshed. Awareness assumes the form of its own creativity. It seems to disappear into its own activity.

In turning back to become aware of itself, it becomes disentangled from activity. The simple experience of just being is awareness minus the content.

The mind cannot do or learn something in order to find awareness. The mind is itself a limitation, a refraction of the very awareness it is searching for and *with* which it is searching.

Anything the intellect does or creates is just more activity in which awareness gets lost. When golf becomes a struggle, this creation of the intellect, by the intellect, is the cause.

When you start *trying* to get out of your own way, the struggle gets harder, not easier.

I speculated earlier that the reason why awareness does this might well be unknowable for the human mind. But the fact that it happens suggests there might be a purpose, *a telos*. (We will explore this idea in a later chapter.)

Perhaps the same telos is at play when a mistake is made, when a golf shot is created that doesn't fulfil your expectations. The initial response will probably be emotional – anger, frustration, disappointment. The ego had decided what was required in that moment. Reality had another idea.

But a poor shot creates an opportunity – to learn and improve. Again, we need to look to direct experience rather than belief. When do you learn more from a game of golf? When everything goes well? Or when the golf course or the conditions get the better of you?

Elite players often bounce back from a loss or a disappointment. They go away and reflect. They practice and develop the skills to meet the challenge next time.

Played from this perspective, every game of golf becomes a win-win situation. You succeed, which is OK. Or you learn something, which is also OK.

Would approaching the game in this way reduce the fear of bad golf shots and other mistakes that make the game such a trial for so many?

Who is more likely to know what is needed right now – your ego, or the wisdom of universal consciousness?

In your experience, what is easier? Going with the flow of reality? Or fighting and resisting it?

The Source of Creativity

When you asked *Am I aware?* in an earlier chapter, it might have been apparent that for awareness to remain with itself can be a challenge.

We are so accustomed to noticing thought and feeling, to seeking and resisting, that attention soon wanders back out towards objective experience, to our perceptions of 'the world'.

As a world of objects is created, simultaneously, a separate witnessing subject also appears.

By simply asking again *Am I aware?* you can encourage the mind to ignore any perceptions and sensations it might be drawn towards, to turn back to its origins once more.

As it embarks on this directionless journey, it sinks or relaxes inwards. It is a colourless, shapeless, indescribable, non-objective experience. It is the experience of a mind that has shed its limitations, that has been divested of finite qualities.

This experience cannot be recalled by the mind because the mind is not there to experience it. Therefore it always feels fresh and unique to go back to awareness.

A mind regularly refreshed by dissolving back into its source is a mind that upon resuming its limitations, is more peaceful, more relaxed, more insightful, and more creative. The discarding of old concepts, theories, and patterns of thought brings new possibilities and insights into whatever theatre or sphere in which the mind might operate.

This refreshed mind will likely feel less tired, less fatigued, youthful, and more alive.

The source of creativity is awareness. By knowing and understanding the nature of awareness, and thus the nature of experience, that innate creativity is allowed to flourish, thrive, and manifest in the world of form.

Whether on the golf course, at work, or at home, the source of creativity is always available. Insight – fresh, original thinking – can spring from this source at any moment to solve problems, create amazing solutions, and point towards happiness.

All we need to do is trust in the potentials inherent in awareness.

The essence of creativity is non-doing.

Creativity naturally unfolds when you are out of your own way.

Key Points from Chapter 8:

- Many golfers are reluctant to explore their innate creativity on the course. They believe that being more mechanical, rather than embracing an artistic approach to the game, will bring success.
- Our culture is based on 'doer-ship'. On individual responsibility and achievement. But the ultimate source of creativity is overlooked when credit or blame is apportioned.
- Awareness is the only certainty. It is the only aspect of experience we can be sure of. It is the knowledge on which all other knowledge is based.
- You cannot decide beforehand when you will be inspired. You can't choose when a creative thought will arise. (Although it would be nice if we could!)
- In knowing itself, awareness assumes the form of the finite mind, and the familiar world of subject and objects arises.

- Golf is a game of mistakes. Mistakes create learning opportunities. This perspective makes every game a win-win situation.
- Awareness is the ultimate, sole source of creativity. 'You' are a creation of awareness.

CHAPTER 9

The Most Consistent Thing You Know

The things you really need are few and easy to come by. But the things you can imagine you need are infinite and you will never be satisfied.

Epicurus

It's a familiar request when someone enquires about coaching:

'I just wish I could play more consistent golf. Can you help?'

When asked to describe the problem, they will usually recount difficulties playing their best golf when it really matters, and their bewilderment and frustration at the chasm between their best shots and their most destructive ones.

This is a tricky situation for instructors who primarily teach the physical side of the game. Because once the fundamentals of the golfer's setup and mechanics of the swing have been acquired, the most common reason for wayward golf shots are errors in the sequencing of the movement.

Timing – as it is often referred to.

As noted in my other books, there is no such thing as a 'pressure-proof' golf swing. The most technically correct golf swing is still dependent on timing. Golf swings don't break down under pressure. As I hope is becoming clear, golfers who attach their wellbeing to outcomes and results are more likely to experience the bodily sensations associated with 'pressure'.

A fight or flight reaction triggering a big dump of adrenaline and cortisol into the limbic system can compromise the sequencing of even the most grooved, well-rehearsed movement pattern. Rushing, or a momentary hesitation at a crucial part of the swing can mean the clubface is open or closed in relation to the target at impact. The ball ends up yards from the fairway or green.

Despite advances in technology available to golf instructors and coaches, timing seems to be a skill it is nigh-on impossible to teach.

The best an instructor can do is encourage awareness of what a well-timed golf swing feels like, and to help the player recognise the difference in a poorly timed one.

Technologies such as the Tour Tempo System

invented by John Novosel are useful tools to enhance this awareness, in the same way that launch monitors provide feedback to improve a golfer's awareness of swing path, angle of attack and clubface orientation.

Human beings seem to have an innate ability to tune into the patterns, regularities, and vibrations of nature. Watching a young child playing on a swing demonstrates how easily the sensation of a pendulum motion can be appreciated.

Your body is tuned into these natural rhythms. Your walk has its own cadence, as do your heartbeat and the way you breathe. I'm reliably informed that being a good dancer has more to do with a feeling for the music than knowing the correct steps and moves.

These observations are surprising only if you consider yourself to be 'other' than an integral part of nature. Something separate, something differentiated and disconnected. Unfortunately, this view is prevalent. Our cultural viewpoint is that there are human beings, and then there is everything else, commonly referred to as 'the environment'.

An example of how understanding yourself as awareness is most important for not only playing the game, but living in harmony with nature too.

The Most Consistent Element of Experience

At the time of writing the *Three Principles of Outstanding Golf*, I saw awareness as an attribute that I possessed or an activity I did. It was personal to me rather than being a universal principle in the way Syd Banks described it. In the months after the book was published, I saw more clearly what Syd was pointing to.

Awareness, or consciousness allows us to be aware of experience. It would not be possible to have the experience of the golf swing without being aware. Being aware is the primary element in *all* experience.

It is always present, constant and consistent. The *content* of experience, on the other hand, *is inconsistent*. It changes moment to moment, it comes and goes. It is temporary, fluctuating, and ephemeral.

But awareness is uninterrupted, it is always aware.

The perception of the fairway in front of you, the feel of the grip on your driver, the sound of a crisply struck iron shot, the smell of freshly mown grass, the memory of the three-putt on the last green, the real or imagined feeling of winning a major championship.

All are known or experienced *via awareness*.

If your wish is to play your best golf more often, would it not make sense to become more in tune with the most reliable element of your experience, rather than chasing and trying to pin down what is always changing?

Firstly, understand that consistency will never be found, because it was never lost. How can you find that which you always are?

Rather, the sense of permanence, your grounding, just gets obfuscated by the activity of the mind as it searches for something already possessed. Like the little old lady searching for the glasses perched on the top of her head.

If you want to experience a natural, innate reliability in your golf game, your *personality* – the story about who you think you are or want to become – must be relinquished.

This narrative has changed many times over the course of your life. Or so it seems. But the story of your 'life' as a succession of events and experiences playing out over time, and the meaning you ascribe to it, only exists in memory and imagination.

When you see that this story is not who you really are, the stability of your true nature is revealed.

Thoughts, Feelings, and Perceptions

Whether you are excited about playing a famous golf course, anxious about a first tee shot, frustrated at a fluffed chip, or angry at an inconsiderate playing partner, you are *aware* of those thoughts, feelings, and perceptions.

Whether you are playing, practicing, putting, chipping, working out, or enjoying a drink at the 19th hole, you are aware of the sensations, of the movements, the sights, the sounds, smells, and tastes.

Whatever you are doing, you are aware of what is being known or experienced as the content or activity of that experience.

Knowing, or awareness, is the continuous background to the ever-changing flow of information, thinking, feeling, and sense perceptions.

Even when you are fast asleep, awareness is present. How else could a sudden noise or movement, or something happening in a dream wake you?

No other element of your experience is continuous, unbroken, unchanging, and consistent.

All other elements of your experience are in flux.

Next time you watch golf on television, notice the screen. The images upon it change from moment to moment. They appear and disappear, the action ebbs and flows, but the screen is a constant.

Thoughts, feelings, perceptions, and sensations may change a hundred times during a round of golf, but the knowing of them, the awareness by which they are known is constant, consistent, permanent.

What you know *about* the game always changes and develops. You are probably a more knowledgeable golfer than when you began playing.

CHAPTER 9: THE MOST CONSISTENT THING YOU KNOW

The knowing *of* the game never changes.

Just Remember

So how might recognition of the consistent nature of awareness help to hit more good shots and fewer bad ones? How does it help you maintain equilibrium and optimism when ambitions and expectations are thwarted by circumstances?

How does understanding true nature help you stay out of your own way?

The first step is to appreciate that being of being aware isn't difficult, or inaccessible, nor does it require a special technique or strategy. The most consistent thing you know – awareness (and awareness of awareness) – is available to anyone at any moment.

Awareness isn't the preserve of the great golfers, wise coaches, or enlightened sages. It is there in the background of every experience every human being ever has, just waiting to be noticed. It is the most ordinary thing.

All you need to do is remember.

Just as the television screen is obfuscated while watching the drama of the final round of the Masters unfold, so awareness gets lost in the drama of your thoughts, feelings, perceptions, and activities as you play on your home course.

Knowing, or being aware, does not rely on the content of experience. It is there in the anxiety of an opening tee shot. It is there in the frustration of hitting a ball out of bounds with a good score going, and it is there during the elation and celebration of holing the winning putt.

Awareness is never modified or changed by the nature of your experience, whether judged good or bad. It is the permanent, stable element in everything you ever do. It is fundamental to experience. It is the only element of experience that can never be removed from it.

In the heat of competition, when the gap between thoughts gets shorter and your feelings and emotions flow like a racing tide, looking past the feelings to the neutral, reliable, consistent awareness *of* the feelings can help you regain perspective. There is no attachment to them.

As you come back to the present moment the chance of following one bad shot with another is reduced. An isolated error or unlucky break doesn't turn into a card-wrecking run of bad holes.

Awareness – The Great Equaliser

Although awareness, or knowing, is not itself an objective experience in the way that a thought, feeling, sensation, or perception are all objective experiences, you can be aware that you are aware.

CHAPTER 9: THE MOST CONSISTENT THING YOU KNOW

(The self-reflective metacognition referred to in earlier chapters.)

Being aware of being aware could be described as the non-objective element of experience. It is that which makes having an experience possible, but it is not itself an experience.

It is the most overlooked element of experience, yet at the same time, the most obvious. There are no special skills or capabilities required to become aware of being aware. You don't need a certain level of intelligence or learn a technique or strategy.

The awareness that Tiger Woods, Rory McIlroy, John Rahm, Georgia Hall, and Lexi Thompson are aware of is the same awareness that you and I are aware of.

The awareness that Hagen, Jones, Hogan, and Snead were aware of, is the same awareness that all the golfers yet to be born will be aware of.

There is one awareness, one consciousness playing as many.

No more effort is required to be aware of it than to notice the screen when you are watching your favourite golfer on television. It is similar to the 'back in the room' experience when you realise you have been totally immersed in a film or TV show.

You don't need to manage, clear, or control your thoughts, notice your breathing, repeat a mantra, or be in a particular feeling in order to be aware of the experience of being aware. Whatever mood or emotion you are experiencing, the possibility of becoming aware of being aware is always available.

When you allow the experience of being aware to come to the foreground and let the thoughts, feelings, perceptions, and sensations recede into the background, something magical happens.

You uncover a peace and happiness that was always present, but was going unnoticed.

You don't need to embark on a great search to find this security and confidence. You don't need to travel to the mountains, sit on a mat in posture, or consult a teacher or guru.

It is available to anyone at any time. As such, it is acknowledged by all major spiritual traditions as the great equaliser, the universal element of the human experience.

It is common to us all, regardless of race, gender, age, intelligence, physical fitness, material wealth, or golfing talent.

When your thoughts are churning and feelings are running amok, timing the swing becomes harder. Good golf seems more difficult. It is normal to look outside to your experience for the reasons for those feelings.

Doing so, however, causes you to think more. The

identity of the separate self is strengthened. Feelings of lack, self-doubt, and insecurity arise. Fuel gets thrown on the fire.

Although hard to recognise in the tension and raucous atmosphere of a big tournament, there is an alternative. By turning away from experience and looking towards awareness, thinking slows down.

The ego settles.

The gaps between thoughts get longer. The blaze is starved of fuel and it dwindles and dies.

There Are No 'Levels of Consciousness'

Awareness is the ultimate constant. It is the most consistent thing you know. It is the source of all experience. It never changes. It is infinite and eternal.

There are no 'levels of consciousness'. Contrary to what you might have read or heard, there is no optimum state of mind from which human beings play their best golf.

You are equally capable in any state of mind if you understand what is going on and let your thoughts and feelings be.

For centuries, human beings have tried different techniques and strategies to will themselves into a state of mind from which they believe a consistently high level of performance would be achieved.

The very idea that such a state is necessary, or

desirable is enough to dramatically reduce your chances of ever finding it. Constantly monitoring your state of mind and comparing it to an imagined ideal, relies upon identification with the ego, the separate self.

Who or what is it that judges the present moment and compares it with a memory of a previous one?

Who is responsible for which thoughts and feelings arise within awareness?

This seeking frame of mind reinforces the subject-object paradigm. The illusion that someone needs to do something. The ego sets itself up as the monitor and judge of what thoughts or feelings are appropriate in the moment.

Pure experience is filtered through a mesh of preconceived concepts, biases, and beliefs.

This obstructs awareness of being aware.

This is the feeling of 'getting in your own way'.

The implications of understanding the nature of the human experience – and the subsequent cessation of searching and seeking – are profound.

The fear that a particular feeling, or lack of one, might cause an inferior performance diminishes. Nothing needs to be done to improve your state of mind so that you might play better.

Consciousness Is Consistent

The more you look to awareness and away from the content of your experience (your thoughts, feelings, and perceptions), the more consistent your golf will become.

Why? Because there is nothing more consistent than awareness. It never changes, varies, fluctuates, or evolves.

It is always the same.

Your experience changes all the time, but the awareness with which you experienced life and golf when you were a child is the same awareness with which you experience it now.

It's the same awareness through which you first became curious about this strange game of hitting a small ball with a weighted stick. And the same awareness with which you will bend over to pick your ball from the cup on the 18th green for the final time.

When searching the content of experience to explain your level of performance, you are looking at a projection of your state of mind.

Experience is real. But the objects of experience, those which make up the game of golf, are modulations of the same awareness with which you are experiencing them.

Your feelings and emotions around the game can

seem so up and down.

In contrast, the awareness by which those feelings and emotions are known never fluctuates. When you are aware of awareness – the primary element of experience – it's impossible to be in your own way.

It is always the same. Constant, reliable, and always available, both on and off the golf course.

What could be more consistent than that?

Key Points from Chapter 9:
- Most golfers seek consistency through perfecting the technique of the swing. But timing has a big effect on the outcome of every shot.
- Awareness is the most consistent aspect of experience. It is always the same. The content of experience is ever changing.
- Your thoughts, feelings and perceptions of the game always change. Awareness of them never does.
- Awareness is not a skill – something to be practiced or developed. It is available the moment you remember who you are.
- Your awareness is the same awareness as the legends of the game were aware of. Awareness is universal – the great equaliser.

CHAPTER 10

Understanding Concentration

*'Fascination is the true mother of discipline.
And Gowf is a place to practice fascination.'*

Shivas Irons in *Golf in the Kingdom*,
by Michael Murphy

MOST GOLFERS SAY THEY WOULD like to experience deeper concentration or focus. Many believe that learning how to control or direct attention is essential to improving performance.

We all know the feeling of being disturbed by our own thinking, of not being present when facing an important shot. This is what many golfers are referring to when they talk about getting in their own way. They assume they have allowed something to distract them. Or have distracted themselves.

Again, before trying to eliminate or prevent distractions, perhaps we should understand the nature of who or what is being distracted?

The word *attention* comes from the Latin *a*, meaning 'to' or 'towards', and *tendere*, meaning 'to stretch'.

It implies the extending or steering of awareness outwards in one predetermined direction.

This is what is being described when attention is paid to an object, activity, or experience. Concentration is regarded as stronger, more intense directing of the same attention.

When you step onto a golf course, attention might be drawn to any one of many features or objects within the environment. There are greens and fairways, tees and bunkers. Trees, bushes and areas of deep, rough grass and scrubland define the playing area.

There might be hills in the distance, rivers and ponds in the valleys, birds, animals, and probably other golfers. Up above, the sun and sky, perhaps some clouds. You feel the wind on your face and notice birdsong.

Your most persistent and intensive attention is reserved for the essential elements of the game: the club and ball, the flagstick and hole.

There are times when you may be so fascinated by one or more of these objects that, to all intents and purposes, nothing else exists.

But what is really happening in these moments of exclusive attention? How do they come about? What is the intention when willing ourselves to concentrate or knuckle down, or when we berate ourselves for allowing attention to wander from the task at hand?

It seems unlikely that concentration can be mastered without understanding the fundamental nature of awareness itself.

Awareness is the Source

As the sun shining on something illuminates it, so awareness is the light that allows an object, thought, feeling, or sensation to be known.

The sun need not shine light on itself; it is the source of light.

In the same way, awareness need not direct the light of its knowing towards itself, the source. What happens if you try to take a step towards or away from yourself?

It can't be done because wherever you go, there you are.

To understand the tension encountered when attempting to focus or concentrate – or indeed to get out of your own way – this paradox must be addressed.

For any knowledge or experience to be known, there must be a knowing subject standing apart from the object or activity.

For example, the golfer (subject) stands separate from the ball (object).

Attention is a word used to describe an apparent connection between subject and object. This is the relationship by which all conventional knowledge and experience is known. It is the world experienced when we play golf or do anything else as a human 'being.'

This is duality.

If you don't understand the nature of awareness, you can waste hours on the golf course, or driving range, or putting green attempting to manipulate or control the very awareness you and the object or activity experienced arise from.

The thought arises 'I must concentrate on *something*' – maybe your golf club, movement of a particular body part, the golf ball or the target. But simple awareness of awareness itself is overlooked.

The problem is not that you are easily distracted and you need to get better at focusing. The entity believed to be doing the concentrating, and that which it is concentrating upon, do not actually exist in the form described by our current model of reality.

In fact, they are both just modulations, or refractions, of the same infinite consciousness. They are illusions of the mind, created by the mind, itself a creation of awareness.

The duality experienced is a mirage.

CHAPTER 10: UNDERSTANDING CONCENTRATION

Falling into Flow

All my life, I've sensed that willing myself to focus or concentrate doesn't improve my performance, or my enjoyment. Trying hard to concentrate seems to take me further away from the present, calm, confident, effortless engagement I drop into when I'm just playing freely. Maybe you've noticed this too?

Worrying about distractions and trying to work out why maintaining attention on a single object or activity is so hard might just be stopping you playing the golf of which you are capable.

A prime example of golfers getting in their own way.

After all, you don't wilfully concentrate or direct yourself to focus during other activities you enjoy and/or have mastered. For example, a fulfilling task at work, another hobby or sport, driving a car, following the plot of a film or book, or preparing a meal.

There seems just the right amount of engagement for the task to be performed naturally and effortlessly, without forcing or striving. 'Optimum grip' seems to be the current fashionable phrase to describe the experience.

Falling into a state of concentration requires the same amount of effort as falling asleep.

Does willing yourself to focus on your golf

swing – something you perform well, such as, make the movement more effective? Does this gross, brutish form of attention help you to play to your potential? Try this 'forced focus' next time you are brushing your teeth or walking up stairs.

What happens?

As observed by philosopher Alan Watts:

"You cannot concentrate, and at the same time, try to concentrate."

What is a Distraction?

I hope by now the fact that you don't choose what you think about or what you focus upon is acceptable. Inner conflict only occurs when you feel your attention has been diverted from where it was meant to be.

A loss of focus or concentration is experienced as an increase in separation between the subject (the imagined separate self) and the object or activity it has chosen.

You will feel you have been distracted by 'something' other than what your mind had decided should be the sole object of attention.

Notice how awareness naturally gets drawn to the most interesting thing in the environment, whether that is a perception (external) or a thought (internal). This may or may not be the thing your

CHAPTER 10: UNDERSTANDING CONCENTRATION

mind had previously selected as the 'correct' focus of attention. Remember, the content of experience is in constant flux.

The gap to the distraction reduces as the distance between you and the desired focus gets longer.

When concentration is experienced, the opposite is true. If you aren't aware of something, to all extents and purposes, it doesn't exist.

When playing well, something might be happening close by, a noise or a movement perhaps. But because you were fully engaged in what you were doing, the disturbance didn't enter your awareness and you barely noticed it, if at all.

A playing partner apologises for rattling clubs or dropping the flagstick, and it comes as a surprise.

You can only be distracted if you believe that you control where your attention is going. If you have a fixed, predetermined idea about where it *should* be pointed.

Flow, or 'The Zone'

Focus and concentration are modulations or activities of awareness. The concept of 'I, the golfer' – a separate self – is a modulation of the same awareness or consciousness.

So too is the object or activity being focused upon.

The typical misunderstanding about awareness as

a personal activity, as *'something I am doing'*, can be clearly seen.

You are aware of the feeling of single-pointed attention as a phenomenon, but is this something *you* are doing? Or not doing? You are aware of the phenomenon of the breeze on your face on a warm day, but you would never think *'I am doing the breeze'*.

The mind trying to focus awareness or to concentrate is like a whirlpool in the river trying to become water.

It is already what it is attempting to become.

Whenever a state of focus or concentration is experienced, it happened effortlessly, without any deliberate 'doing'. The sensation is of a merging, of becoming absorbed into the activity or with the object.

Something interesting is noticed. Curiosity draws attention closer. Other aspects of experience (distractions, as we might call them) fade into the background. Fascination follows.

Time, space, and the sense of self disappear as 'you' forget the story about what is happening and become totally absorbed in the experience.

This is the 'flow state' so highly valued by golfers and coaches.

The separate self seems to evaporate and dissolve into whatever is happening or being observed. There

CHAPTER 10: UNDERSTANDING CONCENTRATION

is only the present moment unfolding.

In 'the zone,' performance feels effortless. It's a relaxing back into the source of experience. Nothing feels easier or more natural.

You only recognise concentration or focus – total immersion in what you were doing – after the fact, when the separate self reasserts itself.

The moment you notice 'I'm in the zone', you are out of it. When the 'I thought' arises, the zone experience is over.

Following their greatest performances, you often hear top athletes often comment that they find it difficult to remember what they were doing or how they were doing it.

There was no separate 'self' present to allow recollection of what happened.

When immersed in the process of playing your best golf, the separate self loses its identity. It has dissolved back into the field of infinite consciousness from which it emerged. It has become one with the game.

It feels like there is no separation from the activity. The word sometimes used to describe the absence of separation is *love*.

This is the ultimate golfing experience. The one we hark back to when the game seems a struggle. Love for the game is the recognition of this experience. A recollection of having played to our potential – the game just flowed.

Trying to Focus

Telling yourself (or instructing someone else) to focus or concentrate is as effective as telling yourself to calm down or relax.

When 'you' attempt to take control of a naturally unfolding phenomenon, you are inevitably reinforcing the illusion of the separate self (subject), and of separate things (objects) and activities. Of duality.

The illusion of the subject-object relationship is founded in the materialist-matter model of the world.

In this case: 'I' or 'you' (the subject) will focus awareness or attention on that thing or activity (the object).

The more you try to concentrate, the more intensely the separate self directs its desire towards the object, and the more distinct and detached from your true nature you feel.

Feelings of insecurity, self-doubt, or anxiety arise. Love for the game evaporates as seeking and resisting take over.

When you forget your true nature, your essential being becomes infused with the limitations of objective experience. You place yourself in the story you are telling, rather than remembering that you are that which knows the story.

You feel limited, isolated, and alone.

It seems like you should have the capacity to direct your attention, to focus or concentrate on the objects in the story. Or on one of the thoughts, feelings, or sensations that you may become aware of as you play. And that doing so exclusively will bring about the desired outcome, and the missing freedom and confidence will be restored.

But this directing of attention away, reinforces the illusion of duality. The illusion that 'I, the subject' and 'it, the object' are separate and distinct in both time and space.

It isn't so.

Why Would Consciousness Limit Itself?

The experience of an ego, or separate self, is the normal, inevitable consequence of interaction with the world of form. In assuming the role of subject, the ego forgets the formless essence of its true nature, your true being.

This is the root of the feeling of struggle, of striving, of getting in your own way.

It's the price that consciousness pays to know the world of thoughts, feelings, sensations, objects, and activities.

Again, the obvious question from the mind is *Why?* Why would consciousness choose to limit itself in this way?

The mind can only guess or surmise, adding a new dimension to the story. We will explore the question of meaning in the third part of the book.

I suggested earlier that the purpose of all games is twofold. Mastery of the game is intrinsically satisfying. But mastery of oneself is even more so, perhaps because it is relevant in all aspects of experience – of life.

And before the art of living can be mastered, you must truly understand yourself, your true nature.

So here is my best guess in response to the question that the mind cannot answer:

If self-knowledge is the ultimate telos or purpose for the fragments of consciousness arising as the form of human beings, couldn't an argument be made that this is equally true for universal consciousness?

Meta consciousness – awareness of being aware – is a phenomenon within nature. As far as we know, only human beings have evolved this dimension of experience. Meta consciousness is the aspect of mentality that allows us to contemplate meaning, indeed for the concept of meaning to exist.

CHAPTER 10: UNDERSTANDING CONCENTRATION

The Illusion of the Ego

Feelings of unease and insecurity that often accompany an attempt to force concentration or focus arise from duality. The separate self is further removed from the true self, the knowing of who you truly are.

Yet awareness is always there just underneath the surface of experience, behind the busyness of seeking and resisting. Feelings of relaxation, freedom, and confidence previously enjoyed can never be completely forgotten.

Indeed, it is the feeling of contentment that the separate self seeks in the outside world.

Occasionally it is experienced again, perhaps after a good shot, during a successful round or tournament. Seeking and resisting end. The separate self dissolves back into its source and becomes one with the activity, or object, or thought.

There is temporary respite from the struggle. The ego retreats. Peace, freedom, and happiness are experienced again.

Unfortunately, the ego associates this feeling with the activity or achievement. It takes responsibility for the result and accepts credit for the performance.

The feeling of flow, of concentration, and of oneness is remembered and added to the list of desirable outcomes, rather than acknowledged as part of the process.

The two illusions are reinforced in the mind. The first being its own existence as a separate entity. The second being the assumption that the good feeling came from what happened.

The truth is overlooked, the seeking and resisting are resumed in the form of trying to focus, or pay attention, or avoid distractions.

Back to getting in your own way again.

When we experience focus or concentration, it isn't something the finite mind has done. It is the relaxing of the separate self back into the source of experience, the merging of the finite mind with the object or activity in awareness.

When this is allowed to happen on the golf course, you have returned to being one with the game you love.

Duality has ended. There is no one to get in anyone's way.

Obstructor and obstructed have become one.

You are back in 'the zone' once more.

Key Points from Chapter 10:
- Most golfers believe that improving their ability to focus would help them play better. This is a misunderstanding about the nature of awareness.
- As with happiness or wellbeing, awareness is not something you do. It is who you are, your essential nature.

CHAPTER 10: UNDERSTANDING CONCENTRATION

- Attention will naturally be drawn to the most interesting aspect or object in the environment. This is subjective.
- 'The zone' is experiencing the absence of the one who is trying to get into the zone.
- Telling yourself to concentrate prevents concentration.

CHAPTER 11

Maintaining Composure

'Tell me who you are Junah. Who in your deepest parts, when all that is inauthentic has been stripped away. Are you your name, Rannulph Junah?

Will that hit this shot for you?

Are you your virtues, Junah, or your sins? Your deeds, your feats? Are you your dreams or your nightmares?

Tell me Junah, can you hit the ball with any of these?'

Bagger Vance, from *The Legend of Bagger Vance*, by Steven Pressfield

RORY MCILROY WON HIS FIRST Open Championship at Royal Liverpool Golf Club in July 2014. Just three days after he lifted the famous claret jug, I was lucky enough to play the course as a guest of my friend Andy Pollock.

I recall standing on the first tee, being struck by the stillness and peace of the famous links after all the activity, excitement, and drama that had played out over the preceding weekend.

Looming out of the early morning mist, the empty grandstands stood as the silent witnesses they'd been to a moment of golfing history. As the golf course is not affected by the drama of the tournament, awareness is never disturbed by the content of experience.

You might feel stressed, under pressure, anxious, frustrated, or angry. You might be tired or in pain. But awareness, the pure knowing by which those sensations are being experienced, is untouched by them.

When one experience transitions into another, no trace is left on the awareness by which the feelings were known.

It isn't a delicate or conditional tranquillity dependent on a technique, a mental strategy, or a reframing of troublesome thoughts. It is a deep, inherent peace that cannot be touched by the drama of whatever experience is playing out within it. It is prior to and independent of the mind's activity.

It is the essence of the composure demonstrated by all the great champions over the decades.

Awareness Is Untouched by Experience

When watching golf on television (to recycle a well-used metaphor) nothing taking place in the golf tournament embellishes or diminishes the screen on which the action appears.

No activity that takes place on the golf course enhances or diminishes the stage on which the tournament took place. Footprints in the morning dew fade away. Grass regrows to heal divots and pitch marks. Likewise, nothing that takes place in experience affects the awareness by which that experience is known.

Awareness is neither improved nor weakened by the acquisition of knowledge, technique, or experience. It is neither refined nor diminished because of anything that happens within it.

Therefore, its nature is peace and calmness. This unlimited sense of resilience and composure is not connected to the condition of the mind, the body, or the outside world. It is independent and innate.

When watching the tournament unfold, absorbed in the action, it might seem like the screen lies behind the images appearing on it. In the same way, when absorbed in the experience of thinking, perceiving, and feeling while playing a round of golf that means something, we might not be aware of awareness as the witnessing presence in the background of that experience.

In becoming more curious about the nature of the screen upon which the golf tournament is being presented, we see that the image is made of the screen. It is entirely permeated by it. Similarly, all experience is saturated with the knowing by which it is known.

Our experience only consists of the knowing of it.

Truth, Beauty and Understanding

Beyond the mind, we instinctively understand that knowing and the experience that is known are not two separate things; rather, they are one and the same. In fact, all there is to experience is awareness.

The absence of separation, otherness, or duality is the knowing of happiness, love, or beauty. Any distinction between subject and object, self and other, is dissolved by this knowing.

Understanding, truth, and beauty are the nature of awareness. When we see, feel, or hear a beautiful golf shot, the enjoyment and satisfaction we experience are actually awareness tasting its own essence, its own eternal reality.

This feeling, this moment, this experience is why we play the game. It is showing us who we truly are.

The question of whether golf is art or science has been a topic of discussion since the game was invented. It might seem that to succeed a player must choose between the two. Trust your instincts and let creativity have free rein? Or work on mechanics, stick to the method, play the percentages?

It might feel as though our personality or character is pulling us in one direction or the other.

The game is taking us to the same place regardless of which path we take. The scientist's search for knowledge is the same quest as the artist's search for beauty and the athlete's pursuit of flow.

Knowledge and understanding are revealed when thinking stops.

Beauty is revealed when a perception comes to an end.

A great golf shot can be appreciated as art or science. The feeling of enjoyment, satisfaction, and fulfilment is the same.

Does Composure Grow with Experience?

The intellect is continually learning, developing, evolving, and changing.

There is a constant flow of thinking, feeling, sensing, remembering, and imagining. But awareness, the primary element of those experiences, doesn't change.

It is never altered, refined, or impaired.

Awareness is not harmed, damaged, improved, or enhanced by any of the experiences a human being might have. It is always original, always pristine, always peaceful, always composed.

No experience, however exciting, troubling, rewarding, or fulfilling, leaves a trace on the pure knowing awareness of that experience.

Your experience of being aware is the same as it was five minutes ago, five hours ago, five days ago, five years ago, five decades ago.

Many of us intuit that although the body might age, we don't feel any different in ourselves than we did ten or twenty years ago. You feel you have always been the same person.

Your thoughts and feelings, personality, and habits of behaviour might have changed dramatically, but the awareness by which they are known has remained the same.

The story evolves and moves on, but the knowing of the story is a constant.

Maybe this is why, as we get older, we find it easier to maintain composure in the face of difficult situations.

Before understanding the nature of awareness, we might put it down to 'life experience' – memories of situations we have known, or the obstacles and difficulties we have overcome.

But as we know, what happens cannot affect or change what we essentially are.

CHAPTER 11: MAINTAINING COMPOSURE

So maybe it's more that we realise the truth of our nature, that it is limitless and invulnerable. And this knowing allows appropriate thoughts and behaviour to arise when the going gets tough.

We get less caught up in the experience itself. Recognition that all the experiences we have had in our lives, both good and bad, have not changed who or what we essentially are.

So, neither will this one.

Composure in Victory and Defeat

The awareness that knows triumph, excitement, satisfaction, and pride at a win is the same awareness that knows frustration, disappointment, hurt, and embarrassment at a loss.

The great players through the ages seem composed in both victory and defeat.

They know that neither experience has the power to affect their essential nature.

They might well shed a tear for a loss, and relish and celebrate their wins. And why not? Knowing who you really are does not mean a numbing of emotions or a denial of feelings. It means embracing the highs and lows and living them fully. Safe in the knowledge that the real you is whole, limitless, invulnerable, and untouchable.

The greatest players of all generations have

acknowledged feeling nervous before a big game. In the preparations and play of an important round or tournament, the ego, or separate self, winds itself up into a heightened state of tension and anticipation.

The bungee cord of attention bounces in many directions as the mind considers and evaluates the challenges of the upcoming event and possible outcomes.

What might this mean for me?

For the ego in this state, anticipation of a loss or a poor performance is a reminder of mortality.

Remember the case of mistaken identity explored in an earlier chapter?

Defeat is a blow to the ego. But it also acts as fuel. The wrong must be righted. The disappointment avenged.

Indeed, the ego's very existence depends wholly on the story it has created about itself matching up with its reality.

The game is played. The outcome is judged. Success! After all the build-up, in the moment of winning a tournament the tension is suddenly released, and the ego collapses back into its source.

All the conjecture that had been spinning around in the mind, dragging the ego from past to future and back again, drops away.

CHAPTER 11: MAINTAINING COMPOSURE

The golfer feels ecstasy and relief, released, and free upon this becoming reacquainted with the present moment and the true nature of his or her own being.

This reunion with its source is the only experience the separate self ever seeks. It craves the destruction of its separate identity and the dissolving back into infinite consciousness from which it emerged.

Every desire that the separate self, the ego, ever really has is this longing for wholeness, disguised as something else – an activity, outcome, or relationship.

It isn't about winning the golf tournament, or the match, or meeting your expectations.

It's about reaffirming the nature of your true being.

It's about remembering who you really are.

After the Victory

Most successful golfers experience this freedom – this diminishing of ego – in playing to their potential, in flow, absorbed in the game, or in the moment of winning.

The feeling of relief and happiness they experience at these times is powerful and addictive. Innocently, they attribute it to the outcome, to the act of winning the tournament. To the apparent security bought by the money. To the recognition, praise, and the justification of all their efforts.

Few really understand what is giving rise to the thoughts and feelings.

After the ecstasy of winning, the separate self reasserts itself by first accepting the praise and taking the credit for what happened. As the pleasure subsides, doubts about whether the success was truly deserved creep in.

The thinking and seeking and striving and resisting resume.

The ego wants more of the feelings of freedom and happiness, so the desire to win again becomes even more powerful. With the increase in expectations, pressure on the golfer at the next big tournament feels more intense. With the next success, the feeling of release is even stronger.

The cycle continues.

'What if it was a fluke?'

'I need to prove myself again.'

'This outcome suggests I'm more capable than I thought.'

'How do I fulfil that potential now? How do I get to the next level?'

Many golfers and other athletes are familiar with the comedown, the empty feeling after the ecstasy of a big win. The illusory separate self re-emerges to fill the vacant space and resumes the seeking and longing for which it exists.

The true goal of sport isn't winning.

If it were, then we wouldn't have the comedown, the feeling of emptiness that sets in soon after.

The true goal of sport is the same as the true goal of life.

The unveiling of our true nature, the knowing of pure awareness felt as happiness and freedom. Relief from the illusion of the separate self and the reacquaintance with the source of experience.

This is why we play.

The Body is Limited, Awareness is Not

As described in Chapter 4, the finite mind – the separate self – derives its sense of existence from the biological structures of the brain or body.

This misunderstanding is reinforced daily by our culture and society, and by experience of a physiology that has yet to catch up with our psychology.

Accordingly, it believes that the referent, 'I', shares the fate and limitations of the body. The mind believes that awareness disappears in deep sleep. But to awareness, it is the finite mind that departs, leaving just pure awareness.

Awareness did not experience its own appearance, its birth. The mind and body were born into awareness. Awareness will not experience its own death; it will continue when the body expires and reintegrates with the earth from which it came.

The body is limited and finite. Awareness is eternal. It remains in the same timeless, ageless condition. Only awareness knows awareness. And in its own experience of itself, it was neither born nor will it die.

Awareness is infinite and everlasting.

The separate self, the ego, rightly believes itself limited and finite. It knows it could come to an end at any moment. This is the nagging sense of insecurity and anxiety with which most golfers are familiar.

The ego thrives on creating a sense of jeopardy or danger. Your self-esteem is on the line in every test or challenge. But the ego also craves the opportunity for aggrandisement, to embellish its credentials. To leave a legacy. To attain immortality.

Some rounds of golf feel 'bigger than' and 'more important than' others because the ego believes you will either be enhanced or crushed by the outcome.

To some separate selves, this feeling of danger, of being under threat of disappearance and then the release from that threat is addictive. The winding up of the tension, the exhilaration, and the subsequent

CHAPTER 11: MAINTAINING COMPOSURE

relief are why some people enjoy exaggerating consequences by betting on the results of a match.

Its why professional golfers want to test themselves at higher and higher levels of play.

All of this is just part of the story of who you think you are.

Just as nothing happens to the screen when we watch a golfer win a great victory or suffer a devastating defeat, so nothing happens to the true self of that golfer in that moment.

It is a great comfort to know your true nature regardless of your life circumstances. In knowing yourself as pure awareness, your composure is always intact.

Awareness – the true self – is invulnerable, imperturbable, infinite, and eternal.

Knowing this truth allows the great golfers to play their best regardless of the situation or circumstances.

When they get in their own way, they fall out of it quickly and without thought.

Composure is maintained through both triumph and adversity, in both victory and defeat.

Key Points from Chapter 11:
- Awareness is untouched by experience. Its nature is unaffected by the experiences – good or bad –

that are known by it. This imperturbability is the essence of composure.

- Understanding, truth, and beauty are revealed when experience comes to an end.
- Composure doesn't come from experience. It comes from the realisation that experience has no effect on who you really are.
- We don't play for the feeling of winning. Winning lets us remember who we really are. The golfer who realises this will rarely lose composure.

Summing Up Part Two
The Implications

Chapter 11 completes the second part of the book. We examined the implications for playing the game from the new understanding described in Part One. A perspective more closely aligned with reality, rather than beliefs. We explored the implications that arise from recognising your true nature in relation to the mental characteristics most valued and sought by golfers.

In Chapter 7, we look closely at confidence, perhaps the most coveted and misunderstood mental aspect of the game. The belief that confidence is a prerequisite for good play is commonly held, but it is another belief not supported by the evidence.

Only the ego, or separate self, can bemoan a lack of confidence. With the recognition of your true nature as awareness comes the understanding that 'you' are OK no matter what happens.

This is true, unshakable, unquestionable, unremarkable confidence.

Recognising awareness as the ultimate source of

creativity is the idea explored in Chapter 8. Many golfers have come to believe that suppressing creativity and emphasising repeatable technique will bring success. This leads to an over-emphasis on control, a fear of making mistakes and of letting go. Our culture is obsessed with 'doer-ship'. With individual responsibility, actions, and achievement. But when credit or blame is apportioned, the ultimate source of creativity is overlooked.

Not understanding the impersonal creative nature of consciousness makes it harder to get out of your own way.

Many golfers seek greater consistency in their game. In Chapter 9, the contrast between the ever-changing content of experience and the constant, reliable, permanent nature of awareness is examined.

Your thoughts, feelings, and perceptions of the game always change. Awareness of them never does. Awareness is not a skill, not something to be practiced or developed. It is ever present, realised the moment you remember who you are.

In Chapter 10, we explore the sought-after but misunderstood phenomenon of concentration. Most golfers believe that improving their ability to focus would help them play better.

This again reveals a misunderstanding of the nature of awareness. As with happiness or wellbeing, awareness is not something you do. It is who you are, your essence.

Your attention will naturally be drawn to the most interesting aspect or object in the environment. We call this curiosity. Curiosity leads to focus. Focus leads to fascination.

To be in the zone is the absence of the one who is seeking the zone. Telling yourself to concentrate ensures concentration will not be found.

Chapter 11 brings us to the end of our consideration of the implications of understanding awareness. Awareness is untouched by experience. Its nature is unaffected by the experiences – good or bad – that are known by it. This imperturbability is the essence of composure.

Composure doesn't come from experience. It comes from the realisation that experience has no effect on who you really are.

We don't play for the feeling of winning. Winning allows us to stop seeking. When seeking ends, the feeling of knowing who we really are is remembered. The golfer who realises this will maintain composure whatever the circumstances.

What to do Next?

After investigating the nature of your experience of the game in the previous chapters, I hope that even if answers to all your questions aren't clear right now, you at least have some tools that might lead to further exploration and will inform your golfing life from this point forwards.

I have no idea how this change in perspective might play out for you. Therefore, to offer advice on how to proceed would be presumptuous. Throughout the book, I have tried to speak from a universal point of view rather than from my own.

As by now you've likely seen, if you understand just one thing, a single universal principle, you can let go of a whole raft of beliefs that were clouding your perspective. This is the power of realising the nature of your own being. From this point on, everything else may start to make sense.

Understanding the nature of consciousness truly is the knowledge that underpins all other knowledge. It is the certainty from which all other relative certainties can be drawn. It is the source of our creativity. The foundations of confidence. The key to consistency. It is concentration. It is the essence of composure.

I hope you have realised from the preceding chapters that you already have access to all these attributes whenever you need them. You don't need to find them or to work at anything for your experience of golf to change.

Just allow your awareness to acknowledge what you already are rather than constantly trying to become something else. Ask yourself, are you moving with the flow of nature, or you are resisting or seeking to change it.

In Chapter 3, I requested not taking anything from this book at face value. I'm suggesting that you use logic and reason to rigorously examine your own beliefs about yourself, about golf, and about life.

Are those beliefs rational? Do they make sense in the light of your direct experience?

The absence of this critical thinking is why so much modern golf coaching is ineffective. Just replacing one set of beliefs with another set doesn't move someone forwards.

You can trust your direct experience through recognising the power that underpins the knowing of that experience. You no longer need to rely on other people's beliefs. And you have a framework within which to question your own.

In the absence of belief, you are free.

PART THREE
What Does Golf Mean to You?

CHAPTER 12

The Search for Meaning

'Man's search for meaning is the primary motivation in his life and not a 'secondary rationalization' of instinctual drives.'

Viktor Frankl – Man's Search for Meaning

IN THE THIRD PART OF THE BOOK, we will further explore how a shift in understanding of true nature might affect the day to day flow of thoughts and feelings.

If you want to put your house in order, you must first take out the rubbish. When it comes to the mental side of golf, the rubbish takes the form of assumptions and beliefs that have accumulated over the years, despite little or no evidence to back them up.

Stripping everything back to the point where you are comfortable with the fact you know nothing for certain beyond your own being, allows a fresh start.

The simplicity of that realisation gets you out of your own way. Slowly your thinking, feelings, and behaviour realign into a solid, reliable mental framework. You stop wasting time and mental energy following trains of thought that just go round in circles.

As with Part Two, this section of the book is optional. If you are playing the game with enjoyment and enthusiasm, feel free to skip to the conclusion. But please remember it's here should your love for the game diminish.

If questions do sometimes arise about why you play, or why your feelings about golf have changed, then I hope the following chapters will help you find answers. They might also help you understand the relevance of the ideas explored in Part One more fully.

The suggestion in the first part of the book is that many of the negative feelings that sap the enjoyment and satisfaction from golf are triggered by the question – implicit or explicit – *What might this mean for me?* Although this is simple enough at face value, as we have seen, major implications arise from that enquiry.

Often, the question is prompted by something in the moment. A poor shot, bad bounce, or unlucky break. A change in situation or circumstance. Anxiety, frustration, anger, or disappointment rises when our expectations are denied in or around the game. These feelings trigger and then feed on the

CHAPTER 12: THE SEARCH FOR MEANING

internal commentary many golfers experience when playing, as referenced in the opening paragraphs of the book.

But if this thought becomes habitual, during a run of poor form or when enthusiasm dwindles, the context can change from a short-term query about responding to the current situation, to a deeper longer-term question.

What does the game of golf mean to me? Leading to others, such as *Why do I play?* If your experience of the game is extended periods of stress, anxiety, and pressure, punctuated by short and infrequent bouts of relief from those feelings, then you may have already given the subject some consideration.

As a thoughtful golfer, you might have wondered whether the game has meaning in and of itself. Why do such strong feelings arise from chasing a small white ball around a field, hitting it into holes and taking it out again, until we arrive back at the place we started?

What are we seeking, expecting, anticipating from participation in this strange endeavour?

The suggestion in the preceding chapters is that the meaning element of *What does this mean to me?* is the wrong place to start when exploring your thoughts and feelings about the game.

Meaning describes your mental models of expected relationships between 'you' and whatever is not you. If you believe you are something you are not, the models of these relationships between your 'self' and everything else will be fundamentally flawed.

So, until you have understood what the 'me' in that sentence is referring to, a better question might be, *To whom does this matter?*

I have (hopefully) put forward a compelling argument questioning the assumption most human beings have about who they really are. Evidence for the entity on whose behalf the question seems to be asked is scant.

If you are comfortable with letting go of this belief, we can return to the question of meaning. What are the implications if relationship with the game is viewed not from the perspective of an illusion – a limited, finite, physical entity – but from the perspective of the true self?

Why Is Meaning Important?

The definition of meaning has been a topic of discussion for Western existential philosophers for about as long as the game of golf has been around (although, surely this is just a coincidence).

The conclusion most have arrived at is a simple one. *Meaning is relation.*

CHAPTER 12: THE SEARCH FOR MEANING

Human beings are meaning-making creatures. Our capacity for metacognition – thinking about our thinking – allows us to imagine connections between objects, identify signals in noise, see patterns in the behaviour of nature, and hypothesize associations in domains where they might not be inherently obvious.

Meaning is what links objects, ideas, feelings, people, and places together in logical and predictable ways. The way most people think about intelligence, is defined, and measured largely by the capacity to identify, understand and make these associations.

We seem compelled to establish these mental models of expected relations, that connect elements of the external environment and aspects of our internal environment, such as thoughts and feelings. Most important, they explain the relationship between the self and whatever is perceived as 'not self' – the apparent outside world.

So, the meaning of the game of golf is an account of the relationships linking the golfer, the course, the equipment used, other golfers, and everything else connected with playing the game.

When we encounter elements of perceived reality that do not fit our established relationship structures, the mental models of *'how things should be or behave'*, we experience feelings of unease, insecurity, absurdity, and discombobulation. (Anyone who has had a putt defy gravity to complete a 360-degree lip-out will be familiar with these feelings.)

Feelings of boredom or disillusionment are often the first signs of a change in or loss of meaning. *'This doesn't make sense anymore.'*

Similar thoughts will be familiar to a golfer who has fallen out of love with the game. Whatever mental model was established to explain the relationship between themself and the game, has now eroded to the point where spending time, energy, and money on it no longer seems reasonable.

Only when that mental model is replaced with another will feelings of enthusiasm, comfort, satisfaction, and enjoyment be regained.

In the final chapter of my previous book, *Take Relief*, I tentatively explored the *Why do I play?* question. For many golfers (for a long time, me included), the meaning of the game lies in trying to prove something, either to yourself or to others. This is what people are alluding to when they speak about enjoying the challenge of the game.

The realisation that the entity you were trying to prove it to doesn't exist is the moment the air comes out of the balloon. The feelings of tension and anxiety, interspersed by relief and satisfaction that were the ever-present background of the experience, disappear as the cycle of seeking and resisting loses momentum.

CHAPTER 12: THE SEARCH FOR MEANING

But then you are left with a gap. Your mental model describing the meaning of the game has gone. And the motivation to play, practice, and improve goes along with it. Unless you can re-establish meaning – come up with a new framework to describe, guide, and motivate your relationship with the game – then chances are your clubs will be on eBay before too long.

A realisation of your true nature is not the most common reason for a loss of your golfing mojo. It more usually happens when you're playing badly, or you stop enjoying the challenge of getting better, or when you are playing too much, and the game feels stale.

It can happen as a natural part of the ebb and flow of life, where other things become more important and your enthusiasm is drawn towards them rather than to the golf course.

The following paragraphs are an attempt to help those who have fallen out of love with golf and are asking the tough question:

Why do I play this stupid game?

Once again, the standard disclaimer applies. Do not take any of what follows at face value or adopt any of the suggestions without bearing in mind the earlier chapters. What someone else thinks about the meaning of the game is irrelevant. It's down to every golfer to find it for themselves.

Conflicting thoughts might arise upon reading that statement. After all, I have spent the whole book pointing away from the personal and towards the universal. Yet here I am seemingly suggesting you find your own reasons for playing the game. The contradiction is glaring.

Through examining and questioning these reasons, I hope the relevance of the ideas put forward in Part One will become clearer. Part Two explored *how* the game might be played from knowing who you really are. This section is about understanding *why*.

In exploring the two different contexts, the difference between the voice of the personal (the intellect) and the whisper of the universal (true nature) will become more obvious.

The Meaning of Life

For thousands of years, up until the seventeenth century when materialism became the dominant story about the nature of reality, human beings seemed to be aware that the meaning is found in transcendence, in rising above the physical limitations of day-to-day existence. Ancient myths and fables point to a deep intuition that each of our lives is a small but fundamental element of something much greater.

Whatever 'it' is, we come from it and will eventually return. The dimension of mystery that still seems an essential aspect of our experience was acknowledged and celebrated by all the recognised spiritual traditions.

Back then, we didn't know very much. And metacognition allowed us to know that we didn't know. In the absence of evidence, it was accepted that the true meaning of existence was probably unverifiable. It couldn't be explained with language, but it could be known through intuition and inferred and communicated through metaphors and symbols.

Then science came along. Any theory about the nature of human beings had to fit models that could be qualified by experimentation or explained with facts.

Instead of using story and allegory as means of passing on intuitive knowledge and wisdom metaphorically, we became increasingly wedded to the literal, to the material, to the correspondence theory of truth. More importance was given to the logic of Aristotle than the logic of inner wisdom and gut instinct.

Towards the end of the nineteenth century, the successes of industry and the political influence of academia allowed the belief that science had everything figured out to flourish. The media of the day promoted the idea that we really understood what reality was and our place within it. Intellectual knowledge was rewarded, certainty was celebrated.

Mystery and doubt were regarded as inconveniences that could be ignored until science provided answers.

This philosophical hubris had the effect of eliminating meaning from our lives, and we are still stumbling around trying to replace it.

Fewer people than ever describe themselves as being religious (while acknowledging the word religion means different things to different people.) Perhaps because the ancient texts that used to ground civilisations and societies seem quaint and fantastic when read literally. They might be good stories but seem irrelevant as manuals to guide how modern life should be lived.

It's ironic that atheists and religious fundamentalists make the same foundational mistake, leading to totally opposing conclusions in meaning. Both take the words of the scriptures literally rather than interpreting them metaphorically – as they were written at the time.

Once societies accepted materialism as the ground of reality, the established sense of meaning in transcendence faded away. What greater purpose could there be for an organism not that far removed in evolutionary terms from the dinosaurs?

As we come to see the insignificance of a single human being in the vast universal scale of space and time, feelings of nihilism are hard to resist. The belief that our sentience, consciousness, arises from and

CHAPTER 12: THE SEARCH FOR MEANING

shares the destiny of the brain and body compounds this despair.

This crisis of meaning lies at the root of the epidemic of mental health problems experienced by western societies in recent decades.

But the desire to understand what this strange experience we call 'life' is about seems to be fundamental. The search for a remedy and a new sense of meaning is ongoing in the fields of philosophy and psychology.

The current state of play isn't encouraging. The cult of the individual has become dominant. From a young age we are bombarded with the message that *'your life is about you'*. Your personal desires, achievements, and rights.

Then we discover that materialism, the dominant, most common explanation of what reality is, implies that our lives are totally insignificant in the great scheme of things. No wonder confusion reigns.

The first and simplest reaction is to just do whatever makes you feel better in the short term, regardless of the effect on people and the immediate environment. This attitude and its implications for societies were described in Chapter Four.

As usual, societal norms have crept into the culture of golfers without being examined or questioned. Individual achievements are regarded as more important than participation, learning and enjoying the game. 'The grind' is celebrated as if it were essential to success. Several philosophical theories have been interpreted in ways that feed this enthrallment with personal aggrandisement and celebrity. A couple of the best known are briefly summarised below.

The Ubermensch

The superman – *Übermensch* – was a concept proposed by German philosopher Friederich Nietzsche primarily as a counter to the doctrines and control prescribed by mainstream religion. His writings are hard to understand, even in the original language. As a result, they have been translated and interpreted to fit, or co-opted by certain political movements as justification for some terrible activities and policies.

Instead of suffering in this world in the hope of redemption in the next one, or just indulging in selfish hedonism, Nietzsche suggested that every human being should be motivated by a love of this life and try to better themselves by living according to the highest values. Whenever you hear someone suggesting trying to *'become the best version of themselves'*, they are nodding in his direction.

It's an attempt to find meaning by transcending the current iteration of 'you', the individual, and becoming a new and improved version through doing or achieving something. Sports, particularly individual sports like golf, are fruitful fields in which to seek personal improvement. Striving to become something more than you currently are.

Becoming a better 'you' might be seen as a worthy goal, but it's one that feeds the destructive pattern of seeking, resisting, and striving explored in Part One.

Successful athletes are celebrated and idealised for their exploits on the field of play, only to be criticised and vilified when they fail. Or when their preferences and behaviour in other areas of life doesn't match society's expectations. Deifying human beings has been attempted repeatedly over millennia in many different cultures, and it always seems to end in the same manner.

Another well-known idea has been co-opted and selectively represented, becoming part of the mainstream western cultural narrative. Charles Darwin's theory of evolution by natural selection is a complex thesis that has unfortunately been reduced in the minds of many people to just one element – survival of the fittest.

This has led to the widespread belief that life is a competition, with narrowly defined meanings of success as achievement and attainment for an individual, judged in comparison to how everyone else seems to be doing. The deeper and wider conclusions of Darwin's work, that success of the wider species is what evolution seems to be moving towards, and that collaboration is as important as competition, is overlooked.

Both characterisations of the nature of self, emphasise personal agency, responsibility, and freedoms. These apparent attributes are held in high regard by people who have been successful, judging by the very measures they hold as important. And so, the ideas are celebrated and perpetuated and come to be societal values. The irony that many of the people regarded as 'successful' aren't that happy, is lost.

These theories have affected the culture of golf and impact on the thoughts and feelings of individual golfers. In most common formats, golf is an individual sport, so the ideas perhaps resonate more strongly for those attracted to golf than for enthusiasts of team sports.

Unfortunately, trying to replace the timeless, intuitive meaning of life as transcendence, by becoming a better version of 'you' *the individual*, seems not to be working. There is ample evidence for the futility of this approach in the ranks of renowned golfers, athletes, businesspeople, and celebrities.

They came to dominate their field and are successful, only to find that the happiness and fulfilment they anticipated was temporary.

The ancient stories and fables that guided societies thousands of years ago implied that individual achievement was just a signpost pointing us back to the source. That personal glory was only reflected from the greater whole. As the myths were neglected and forgotten, so was the core understanding.

But the desire for meaning, for fulfilment, still seems to be as strong as ever.

Science has become the new ground of knowledge, and so psychology has become the field in which the search continues.

Key Points from Chapter 12:
- Meaning describes your mental representations of expected relationships between 'you' and whatever is 'not you'.
- Human beings seem compelled to look for meaning.
- Feelings of boredom or a lack of enthusiasm for golf are symptoms of loss of meaning.
- The traditional meaning of life for our ancestors was transcendence.
- This has been lost in recent decades, and we are still searching for an alternative.

CHAPTER 13

A Psychological Theory of Meaning

'To be purposeful is not to be goal oriented, but to seek to reconnect to the source of one's life.

Michael Meade

THE OPPOSITE OF MEANINGFUL IS MEANINGLESS. The feelings most associated with meaninglessness are boredom or the absence of enthusiasm. When an individual loses meaning in a particular aspect of their life, a period of insecurity and anxiety and lack of enthusiasm will ensue until they compensate by finding something else they are passionate about, or by finding new meaning.

Meaninglessness is a recurring symptom of the current mental health crisis that unfortunately afflicts a significant proportion of Western societies, despite our comparative economic advantages.

Meaning describes the mental model of the expected relationship between two objects, or between a subject and an object. So, *What does golf mean to me?* is questioning the relationship between the golfer and the game.

Falling out of love with golf might be dismissed as a minor issue in comparison with symptoms of meaninglessness in wider society, such as addiction, inequality, or the loss of cohesion in communities. But for those individuals who no longer play, it is significant. And golfers are part of that wider society. They will only return to enjoying the physical and mental health benefits the game can bring when new meaning is found.

So, what feelings and insights do you anticipate from the experience of playing? Excitement from contesting a closely fought match. Satisfaction from getting your handicap down? Fulfilment from mastering the challenge of the game? Camaraderie and friendship from playing with regular partners? Recognition and respect from your peers? Peace and relaxation through being outdoors in nature?

A mixture of all of them?

You might have noticed that the game means different things to different people, and one person might have a different relationship with the game at different times in life.

So, does golf have meaning in and of itself? (As a thought experiment, imagine explaining to an alien who had just landed on earth the feelings and sensations experienced by a golfer trying to hole a three-foot putt to win their first major.)

CHAPTER 13: A PSYCHOLOGICAL THEORY OF MEANING

From the perspective of the intellect, the thinking mind, the game means whatever you believe it means. (Worth bearing in mind whenever the thought arises that golf is *making* you miserable.) But if you must 'make meaning,' it's worth considering whether that meaning is 'real'. Or is it just another example of the mind's capacity to deceive itself?

Meaning has become a hot topic in the field of psychology, prompted by issues arising from the mental health crisis already described. Despite scepticism of many concepts that the discipline advances, useful insights into our thinking and behaviour can be found. The literature around meaning contains relevant observations that golfers and the organisations who administer the game might find of interest.

The Meaning Maintenance Model (Heine, Proulx, and Vohs, 2006) is a psychological framework that draws from different studies to propose four domains of meaning. These are self-esteem, belongingness, symbolic immortality, and certainty or closure.

It is proposed that human beings *'fluidly compensate'* between domains. When meaning is disrupted or lost in one, it will be sought in another. The domains are linked and overlap. For example, self-esteem and a feeling of belonging or being valued in a group or culture are closely linked.

Take a moment to reflect on changes in meaning that have occurred over your golfing career, or that you may have noticed amongst your long-time golf companions. Do they correspond to the domains identified above?

Just bear in mind that mainstream psychology (and therefore this model) is firmly embedded in the materialist paradigm. In the next chapter, we will consider whether the conclusions drawn might be interpreted differently in light of the arguments put forward in Part One of the book.

Self-Esteem

According to most psychology models, self-esteem is vital to mental health. It is perhaps the most important construct in our perception of meaning in our lives. It is generally viewed as a measure of success in relating to the external world.

Therefore, it is assumed that achieving a single-figure handicap or winning the club championship will enhance self-esteem. As can a promotion at work or finding the right life partner.

In social groups, self-esteem is derived from being valued by the collective.

'If they think highly of me, then I am justified in thinking highly of myself,' and vice versa. So, feelings of worthiness might arise from being selected to represent your club, county, or country in competi-

tions or from getting compliments about your swing from your peers.

Many young golfers see the game as a path to 'becoming someone.' Success leads to feelings of achievement, of self-worth. Mastering a difficult skill brings intrinsic feelings of satisfaction. It also brings acknowledgement and praise. Success sets you apart but also enhances your standing in the eyes of others.

These patterns of thinking are perfectly valid and normal for an adolescent or young adult establishing their own identity and learning about themself and their relationships with the world. But, as described in earlier chapters, identification with the character in the story can go too far.

If you start confusing who you are with what you do, problems will usually follow. And if your self-worth is derived from epitomising the values of a culture or society, what happens if the values of that society change, or when you realise they might not be grounded in what is true?

Losing self-esteem indicates that an individual is struggling to functionally relate to their environment. For a golfer, not feeling good about yourself might be attributed to a run of poor form, trying to change your swing or game to meet different expectations, unsuccessfully attempting to step up to the next level of competition, or through being unable to play due to injury or other factors.

You might feel that your play isn't good enough to be part of your regular group, or to join up with golfers you haven't played with before.

What happens when you achieve your goals and can't find new ones? Or when your expectations prove to be unrealistic due to age, lack of practice time, or just plain old lack of ability?

The feelings and insights anticipated from playing don't arise. Meaning goes out of the game. Boredom, frustration, or simple loss of enthusiasm are the symptoms. This experience might lead to a reassessment of what the game means to you. Attempts to 'fluidly compensate', to find new sources of self-esteem, will be made. Setting new goals or seeking meaning in other domains are normal responses.

Symbolic Immortality

It has long been recognised that as the years go by, more human motivations reflect the anxiety associated with the eventual demise of the physical body. Thoughts about the inevitable passing of the main character in your story become more relevant.

For most of our lives, self-preservation of your current form is an overriding goal. But metacognition allows human beings to comprehend that failure in this regard is certain. What's the point of struggling and striving to achieve and accumulate if, at some

CHAPTER 13: A PSYCHOLOGICAL THEORY OF MEANING

point, you're going to disappear anyway?

In the materialist paradigm, death and loss of meaning are inextricably linked.

Making sense of this uncomfortable situation becomes more of a priority as the years pass. One way human beings address the anxiety that arises from the acknowledgement that they do not have literal immortality, is through the desire for symbolic immortality.

'Leaving a legacy' is a well-known motivation for champions at the top of the game. The opportunity also arises for players at the local level. Once your name is 'on the board' at your golf club, it will be there for as long as the establishment is in existence. Potentially for hundreds of years if history is anything to go by. The thought that your achievements will still be recognised when you are no longer around can give meaning to your game – and perhaps to your life.

Unlike other sports, a golfing career can be measured in decades rather than just years. But even so, there comes a time when the realisation occurs that the standard of play you were capable of isn't available anymore.

Self-esteem derived from your ball striking, scores, or competition results fades. You can still compete, due to the handicap system. But deep down, you know that the golfer you once were has gone. The meaning of the game might well change, as described in the next domain.

Belonging

Human beings have a strong innate desire to belong. We are pack animals. Cultural and social motivations are significant influences on both thinking and behaviour. We have long recognised that our success as a species and as individuals relies upon forming mutually dependent groups. Belonging and self-esteem are closely linked in this regard.

Participation in team sports is an obvious reflection of this desire. But golf is played mainly as an individual sport. It can therefore be attractive to people who are introverts, apparently less motivated by belonging. Some golfers 'fluidly compensate,' finding meaning in the domain of self-esteem. They become proficient by spending a lot of time playing and practicing on their own. Many fine players over the years have been described as self-absorbed or loners.

But this apparently selfish point of view cannot be maintained. Your achievements and your legacy only have longevity in the culture in which they are valued. If that culture or aspect of society withers and becomes irrelevant, then what are those achievements worth?

In my younger days, I looked at some of the old-

CHAPTER 13: A PSYCHOLOGICAL THEORY OF MEANING

er, less competent golfers at the club and wondered what possible satisfaction they could be getting from playing the game as badly as they did. I didn't understand what golf meant to them. I saw it as an opportunity to derive self-esteem from improving, playing well, and winning.

But for most of them, it came to represent a social experience. A chance to meet with like-minded friends and enjoy some fresh air and exercise in pleasant surroundings. The buzz of some gentle competition with perhaps a bonus of the occasionally solidly struck golf shot or long putt holed.

The quality of ball-striking and the challenge of making a score slipped down the list of what was important to them. They wanted to be remembered as valued golfing companions and stalwart members of the club. To support and safeguard the culture of the game.

Perhaps this is why many former champions often speak about 'giving something back'. Yes, there is an altruistic desire behind their contribution, but also a personal one.

Your achievements mean nothing if the arena in which they were gained disappears. In this sense, the desire for symbolic immortality and the desire to belong are intertwined. If nobody plays golf anymore, what is the significance of Jack Nicklaus's eighteen major championships?

Earlier in the book, I referred to the 'culture of golfers' (a phrase first coined by Fred Shoemaker). Many aspects of this culture are problematic in terms of how we relate to the game. But just by being a golfer, you belong to something greater than you. You have thoughts and feelings in common with other golfers, and you join with them in a shared enthusiasm. This belonging is part of the meaning you derive from playing the game.

Certainty or Closure

The fourth domain of meaning is the desire for closure. Anyone who has gone down the rabbit hole of trying to fully understand their golf swing, or 'own' it, as mastery of the movement is sometimes described, will be aware of the motivating power of the desire for certainty.

Most golfers have felt at some point, *'I've got it!'* The swing thought or concept that (at least for a while) gives them confidence they know where the ball will be going. Unfortunately, this feeling is temporary, even for the best players in the world.

The quest for certainty is why some people stay fascinated with the game their whole lives. No matter how good your last round, there will always be aspects that could be better. No one has ever played the perfect tournament or become the 'complete' golfer. As has been said many times

CHAPTER 13: A PSYCHOLOGICAL THEORY OF MEANING

before, and by people who have played the game better than anyone else, golf is the sport that can never be fully conquered.

But the desire for mastery, for total control, is what keeps the true devotees coming back for more. It is the ultimate challenge of the game.

Any question about *why* is a search for closure. This is true on a micro level – when it comes to understanding why your golf ball does what it does. Notice the train of thought your mind follows after a poor shot (once the anger has subsided.)

'If I can understand why that just happened, I can learn to fix it. With a bit of practice, I won't have to worry about hitting that bad shot again. I will be a step closer to having control and certainty over the outcome and golf, and life will be better.'

The *'I've got it'* thought described above is at the start of a similar train of reasoning but applied to a good shot.

Why? is also relevant on the macro level, as in *Why do I play the game?* It seems that if you can find the ultimate answer to this question, then golf will always be meaningful. It will always provide some opportunity for satisfaction, even when your form deserts you and results are disappointing. If you have a strong belief about why you play, there will be meaning in the struggle to overcome your difficulties and get back on track.

There is meaning in accepting the challenge of the game.

But investigating why you play rarely, if ever, ends in a lasting satisfactory outcome – in closure. As I mentioned earlier, the why question can only be asked on behalf of an entity that does not actually exist. It usually arises from trying to prove something to yourself, or to others.

And as the Meaning Maintenance Model describes, the meaning of the game is a moving target. It will change over time. Attempting to pin it down is a one-way ticket to frustration. Asking why will usually lead to the formation of a belief. And as we have explored in Chapter 3, adding beliefs isn't helpful.

As is often the case, it's useful to recall how we came to play the game in the first place. Most young golfers don't have a fully formed intellectual hypothesis about why they play. It's just something they do because it's enjoyable.

If the purpose of life is to be happy, enjoyment is the best meaning of all. It doesn't require further intellectual analysis or explanation.

Rather than asking ourselves why we play, maybe we should be asking, why not?

Meaning, or Self-Deception?

From the perspective of psychology, the four domains model of meaning is plausible. As is the suggestion that we compensate for a loss of meaning in one domain by looking for it in another. I have noticed that my meaning of the game has changed several times over the past thirty years. The same is true for many of my friends and colleagues.

But something doesn't feel quite right about this theory. It seems incomplete somehow. The more I learn about the nature of the mind, the more aware I become that one of its most persistent and prevalent tendencies is to deceive itself.

The very same capacity for adaptation and creativity is what allows this self-deception. Most psychological techniques and strategies that have been developed over the past 100 years have taken advantage of this tendency. We know that we can alter, and temporarily improve our experience of life by reframing thoughts or replacing one set of beliefs with seemingly more functional ones.

I'm not sure there is a way of escaping this. We are trapped by our own cognitive functioning. We don't interact with reality but with a subjective interpretation of the information brought to us via the senses.

Perhaps the best we can do is to know that it is happening and to treat our own thinking with scepticism rather than taking it seriously as most people do, especially when they are on the golf course. The ability to laugh at yourself is a sign you are getting comfortable with uncertainty, with not knowing.

Realising that you are not your thoughts is a major step in the right direction when it comes to not deceiving yourself. But where does that leave us when it comes to the very real desire for meaning? Perhaps the four domains described above are just stepping stones leading to something more fundamental.

Rather than compensating for an apparent lack of meaning, what if we let go of our preoccupation with the literal? Perhaps play is one way to reconnect with the long-lost meaning of transcendence, through the metaphor of a game.

Play is something that seems intrinsic to human beings and to other intelligent creatures. There have been many theories, most concluding that play is a preparation for something later in life, something functional and utilitarian. But many animals, including humans, seem to play games for the sheer joy of playing.

And maybe playing games such as golf can connect us back to and help us re-establish a deeper, more intuitive meaning of life.

This is what we will explore in the last chapters of the book.

Key Points from Chapter 13:

- *What does golf mean to me?* is a question about the feelings and insights a golfer anticipates from playing the game.
- Many golfers are looking for success as a way of boosting self-esteem.
- Thoughts about leaving a legacy through your achievements in the game can provide a source of meaning as you get older.
- The search for certainty or closure is the main reason many golfers stay in love with the game for their whole lives.
- Being a golfer fulfils a desire for belonging; to a club, to a society, or to the wider culture of golfers.

CHAPTER 14

An Alternative to Psychology

'Life is a laboratory for exploration along only two paths; feeling and understanding. All else exists only as connotative devices: 'tricks' to evoke feeling and understanding. All meaning resides in the emotions and insights unfolding within.'

Bernardo Kastrup, *Brief Peeks Beyond*

SO FAR IN PART THREE OF THE BOOK, we have explored how the innate human desire for meaning overlaps and is woven into the misunderstanding around who we really are.

Unquestioning acceptance of metaphysical materialism and disillusionment with mainstream religion, leaves the field wide open for belief in the sovereignty and primacy of the individual to dominate. In the prevailing culture, meaning is primarily sought in personal achievement and attainment and the accumulation of material wealth.

We are told from a young age that our happiness depends on these things. But even when we get them, peace and fulfilment are fleeting. This in turn has led to confusion and feelings of meaninglessness, which shows up in the mental health crisis and other socioeconomic problems.

The damage this misunderstanding is doing to individuals and societies is being recognised. Cultural norms grounded in this paradigm have prevailed over the past century, but there are signs of hope. Curiosity about alternatives to 'winner takes all capitalism' is growing. The determinism implicit in Darwin's theory is being questioned. The interest in mindfulness and other non-religious spiritual paths suggests that Western thinking might be opening up towards a more enlightened view of the future.

Psychological studies informed by philosophy have connected relevant aspects of our thinking and behaviour, even if the inferences drawn are usually framed from a materialistic rather than from a non-dual perspective.

Let's reconsider the Meaning Maintenance Model to see whether alternative conclusions might be available informed by the understanding explored in Part One.

The True Self and Self-Esteem

The evidence that being successful does not automatically bring lasting happiness and increased self-esteem is more obvious than ever. This can provoke individuals to question the values of the culture they are living in. Numerous well-known golfers and other athletes have reached the pinnacle of their sport, only to find themselves wondering, 'Is this all there is?'

People who have reached the top of their chosen field are often more motivated to enquire into the meaning of life and the nature of reality than those who continue to chase. If you have played the game and won and you are still not content and free from worry, then you have more reason to question the rules of the game than if you are still playing.

The early chapters of the book explained how mental health issues attributed to a lack of self-esteem have their root in the misunderstanding about who we are. Attempting to find contentment by burnishing the credentials of an illusory self through personal aggrandisement makes the confusion worse.

If self-esteem was a goal in itself, achievement would lead to happiness and fulfilment of that desire. The fact that we seem to need to keep topping it up, should cause us to question what that motivation is really pointing towards.

Perhaps an ongoing desire for self-esteem is asking about the true nature of who or what we are? Recognising the 'self' you feel lacks esteem is the key.

If it is the main character in the story of 'you' – something defined, something with a past and a future, something that can be diminished or enhanced (as most psychological models seem to assume) –then we are back to the problems described in earlier chapters.

Realising true nature transcends the need to boost self-esteem or to compensate for lack of it. You find meaning in doing what you love for the sake of it, rather than the activity being a vehicle to get somewhere, or a transaction through which you become something.

You Are Not Limited

The Meaning Maintenance model acknowledges that symbolic immortality motivations are tricky to define as such, mainly because they overlap and merge with other domains of meaning. The desire to leave a legacy, for ongoing recognition is difficult to separate from the desire for self-esteem that comes with achievement today.

As mentioned previously, recognition of those achievements is dependent upon the survival of the culture in which they occurred, so they depend on belonging. When it comes to mortality salience, contemplation of closure or certainty is pretty much the same thing. The only issue is *when* the end comes, rather than *if*.

CHAPTER 14: AN ALTERNATIVE TO PSYCHOLOGY

Injury and age-related loss of speed and power are often what forces an athlete to re-evaluate and reassess themselves and their life. Perhaps from this point of view, golf-career longevity can be a double-edged sword. There is the Seniors tour. You can still be trying to make it as a player in your fifties. Professionals in other sports confront this loss of identity much earlier. They face the existential dilemma of *'I'm not a footballer or a rugby player anymore, so who am I?'* with another thirty or forty years of active life in front of them.

Desire for symbolic immortality fades away with realisation of the infinite nature of awareness. Once you accept that there is no evidence that the awareness you are shares the destiny of your body, then your legacy is simply the fruits of staying out of your own way and enjoying your life; there is no longer pressure to achieve something that defines you.

If thoughts of how you will be remembered bring happiness, then all well and good. But symbolic immortality is irrelevant once you have recognised the limitlessness of your essential nature. Why do you need to leave a mark as proof of your existence to others when there are no others?

You are free to live in the moment instead of suffering the pressure exerted by the confines of space-time. The desire for symbolic immortality is quenched when the ego comes to an end.

The Impossible Game

You can't control all the variables relevant to your ambitions. You can never have certainty. Nature is a complex system. Tiny variables in one input value can lead to wild variations in outcomes. You can do everything right, and still not get what you want, or what you think you deserve. And when we are successful, it seems to be human nature to overlook the role good fortune has played.

There are parallels to be drawn with driving the golf ball. Tiny changes in face angle or centredness of strike can lead to extreme variations in where the ball goes. Ironically, trying to hit the ball straight often makes things worse than trusting your swing and letting the shot go. With practice you get lucky more often, and the ball goes where you hoped. Sometimes, you are unlucky. You end up in the rough, or the woods, or the water. But your mind and body learn from doing. If you gain understanding, then perhaps the momentary disappointment is worth it.

Psychological suffering seems to be the way nature suggests you pay attention to what is important. It forces you to ignore what is trivial, banal, inconsequential, superficial. It tells you when you are taking yourself too seriously. Maybe that's why it seems to be an inevitable aspect of our experience?

Suffering can quickly dispel any ideas 'you' personally have about being in control. You are never in

CHAPTER 14: AN ALTERNATIVE TO PSYCHOLOGY

control; you have never been in control and never will be. In my experience, suffering can point you towards the truth. Relief from suffering and the most satisfying feeling of certainty and closure come from letting go of the need for them. From the realisation that 'you' aren't the one who is suffering, or who needs to know.

In golf or in other aspects of life, the game of mistrust and seeking happiness and well-being in control and certainty is an impossible game to win. It would require being Nietzsche's *Übermensch*.

The desire for meaning in certainty or closure is not fulfilled by thinking you know everything, by having it all figured out. It is suggesting we recognise the only certainty, the knowledge of who we really are. The knowledge on which all other knowledge is based.

Belonging to the Game

The work of an engineer has meaning predominantly for the people who fly in the aeroplane or drive the car they helped to design. The work of an architect essentially only has meaning for the people who inhabit, work in, or visit the buildings they built. The meaning of a scientific discovery is realised in the application and use of the technology that is developed from it. And the writings of an author only have meaning for those who read and enjoy their books. The only true legacy is not in the object or the activity. It is in the feelings you inspired in others.

The achievements of a golfer only have meaning if the game continues to be watched, enjoyed, and played, however well or badly, by other golfers. If the Scottish shepherd had been ridiculed or ignored or had kept his new pastime to himself, then golf as we know it wouldn't exist.

If the game is no longer played, watched, and enjoyed, then the great shots and the achievements of all previous players will be rendered irrelevant. So, in that sense, the meaning of our game is maintained and nourished every time a new player picks up a club for the first time and finds purpose and pleasure in swinging it.

This has significant implications for you and every golfer, regardless of your ability, experience, and proficiency. Every shot you play has meaning. It is essential to the whole game. Every swing you make is fundamental to the tournaments played today by Rory McIlroy, Tiger Woods, and Georgia Hall.

And not only for current players. Without you, the golfer of today, the play, the scores, and the legacies of Old Tom Morris, Bobby Jones, Ben Hogan, Jack Nicklaus, Tom Watson, Seve Ballesteros, Karrie Webb, Annika Sorenstam, and that unnamed Scottish shepherd, mean nothing.

The realisation that every golfer who has ever

played the game is as important as every other golfer points us to a truth about ourselves. You are not separate. We are all fragments of the same whole. The word *universe* means 'all that there is'. It is impossible to deny that you are part of that universe, whatever it is made from and however it came to be.

The intuition that 'the game is bigger than any individual player' resonates deep within. It reminds us we belong to something greater than ourselves. As a player and lover of the game, you are as important to its meaning and existence as every other golfer who has ever picked up a club. The feeling that accompanies this recognition is the true spirit of the game.

Perhaps our desire to belong is a reminder that we always belong, that we are always connected to the source. We are one awareness showing up as many. The desire for belonging might just be pointing us back towards the meaning of life we abandoned years ago.

Identification with the body/mind and the way societies celebrate and champion the individual has distracted us and made it harder to understand meaning. Maybe the games we play, instead of being vehicles for escapism, or ways to fortify the ego, can reacquaint us with the source of true meaning – of transcendence.

Why Do We Play?

When you step onto the first tee, you don't know what is going to happen. If you knew, you probably wouldn't play. Do we love games because they reacquaint us with the unknown, with mystery? Does play allow us to explore the dimension of mystery in relative safety?

Think back to when you were a child. A game creates a situation where jeopardy can be experienced. We compete with our ideas of our future selves, and with others. We can learn about ourselves and about other people from our reactions to the unexpected, our thoughts, and feelings in moments of exultation, and disappointment. We experience altered states of consciousness – the zone, or flow.

There are games within the game. One of which brings us back to the opening paragraph of the book. See if you can recognise the difference between the voice of the impersonal, and the voice of the ego. Is the voice speaking about recognition, achievement, distinction, control, prizes, etc.? Is it coming from a place of insecurity or fear. Who is that?

With practice, you can recognise the difference between your mind searching for closure to compensate for a lack of meaning, and your inner wisdom, the voice of nature suggesting you remain open to all possibilities. The impersonal will never tell you the why. But you can develop trust. You learn that if you

CHAPTER 14: AN ALTERNATIVE TO PSYCHOLOGY

get out of the way and let reality happen through you, it feels good. There is meaning in the experience, even if you can't explain it.

Golf can feel very personal sometimes. Especially when your play doesn't meet prior expectations and your ego isn't enjoying it. But these feelings are telling you something important. They are a reminder you have forgotten what the game is really about. After all, every golfer knows deep down that the game means something more than the individual golfer.

The moment you fall into the trap of thinking it's about you, you are doing yourself and the game a disservice. Because if the game is just about you – about your scores, your results, your shots, and what other people think about you, it has no meaning *beyond* you. When you stop playing, the game will be over.

Understanding what golf means to the people who play has important implications for those who take it upon themselves to 'grow the game'. You don't make it more attractive by making it 'cool', easier, or less time consuming. The game grows when people try it and find meaning in it.

If you want them to keep playing, you help them understand the feelings they had when they first took it up. To help them find new meaning as their golfing life evolves.

Sport is sometimes described as religion for the modern day. People gather in common cause to enjoy, to share an experience, to celebrate. Unfortunately, our society is in danger of making the same mistake with sport as we have with religion. When something is taken literally that is meant metaphorically, confusion ensues. Meaning is lost.

When play becomes all about an outcome and it is taken personally rather than realising what it is pointing us towards beyond the person, we have forgotten what games really mean.

Forget About Why

Mastering the mental side of the game isn't about controlling your thoughts and feelings or coping with them. It's simply about understanding them. When you understand the relationship between thought and feeling, you know that your situation or your circumstances don't have the power to dictate how you feel.

When you understand that you don't control your thinking, you also understand that you don't need to. And when you understand who you really are, you know that the question *What does this mean for me?* has very different implications than if you don't.

When it comes to the meaning of the game itself, if it has meaning, it is the same meaning as that of life itself. If you replace the word *life* with *golf* in the quotation at the start of the chapter, you end up with something that might summarise the discussion in a couple of sentences.

Golf is a laboratory for exploration along two paths – feeling and understanding. An exploration is undertaken in the spirit of curiosity, of doubt, of not knowing. Again, think back to the experience of playing as a child. Did you ever ask yourself why you were playing?

Games can take us to places in the mind that aren't the norm in the routines of everyday life. The zone is an enhanced experience of consciousness. It's where we feel free. A reality more real than real. We connect with others and share experiences with them. We find closure in knowing who we really are. We feel the freedom and happiness that cannot be found in the seeking of esteem for a self that doesn't exist.

Getting out of your own way points to the transcendence our ancestors knew to be the real meaning of life.

Key Points from Chapter 14:
- The desire for *self-esteem* prompts us to remember who we really are.
- The desire for *symbolic immortality* reminds us of the infinite, unlimited nature of consciousness.

- The desire for *closure* reminds us there is only one certainty.
- The desire to belong reminds us we are an essential part of something greater.
- Play gives us opportunities to experience feelings and states of mind less freely available in everyday life.
- Getting out of your own way is transcendence.

CHAPTER 15

Did You Choose to Play Golf?

'I'm not trying to sell you on this idea in the sense of converting you to it. I want you to play with it. I want you to think of its possibilities.

I'm not trying to prove it. I'm just putting it forward as a possibility of life to think about.'

Alan Watts. The Dream of Life

I HOPE THAT THE PREVIOUS CHAPTERS have been helpful if you have at some point wondered why you play the game, or why you feel the way you do about it. But there is another relevant question that sometimes follows:

Why golf?

Why not gardening, or tennis, or computer games, or repairing old clocks, or playing the trombone? The options are endless. If we accept the definition of meaning as a mental model of expected relationships between ourselves and objects or activities, then it follows that similar emotions and insights to those gained from playing golf might be anticipated from participation in any of these other pastimes or hobbies.

So, why did you choose golf ahead of any other possibility?

Or did golf choose you?

Back in Chapter 2, I described the second big realisation I had about the nature of experience and the way the mind really works. From a personal perspective, control over what I think or feel is an illusion. I can't choose what thoughts I want or don't want, or when they arise or disappear. We don't choose who or what we fall in love with.

Therefore, I didn't choose to play golf. Or subsequently decide that I wanted to make a career out of it. If the definitions of and observations about meaning described in the previous chapter are accepted, I didn't choose what golf meant to me at the point any of these decisions occurred.

As I first suggested in *The Three Principles of Outstanding Golf*, and then described in more detail in *Take Relief*, this apparent lack of agency over my mental processes was troubling. It became undeniable the more I explored it. It called into question an aspect of my experience that seemed important, essential to my wellbeing and happiness – the ability to choose my attitude to life.

Free will is one of the most celebrated and hon-

CHAPTER 15: DID YOU CHOOSE TO PLAY GOLF?

oured psychological principles, one that is often linked to meaning. The renowned Austrian psychotherapist Viktor Frankl's 'logotherapy' is based on the pretext that while you cannot choose what happens to you, you can *'choose your attitude in each set of circumstances'*. As a survivor of the Nazi concentration camps, we should certainly take his words seriously.

Yet how can a will be said to be free if there is no control or agency over what is willed? Free will is assumed when it comes to the playing of games. It might be the primary aspect that distinguishes play from work.

It seems like we play because we choose to. Not because we need to, or are forced to.

You Are What You Identify With

As with the hard problem of consciousness described in Chapter 4, the paradox is resolved not with a new discovery or a clever insight but by simply realising a wrong assumption has been made early in the chain of reasoning, leading to the labelling of a 'problem'. When you frame the situation in a different way, or ask a different question, the error becomes obvious. The problem solves itself.

When 'you' identify with the body and with the mind – which together form the individual, disassociated segment of awareness in which your personal story seems to appear – then it seems like 'you' are the one doing the thinking, the one making the decisions, the one who has control, the one who has responsibility for what happens – and your attitude to it.

But as we have seen, this illusion of control is called into question every time you have a thought or a feeling you don't like. Or you find you can't recall something you thought you knew. Or you have an insight, some fresh thinking that surprises and excites.

It is obvious that the entity that approves or disapproves of whatever thought or feeling just arose had no say in the matter of its creation. But the only way that the illusion of personal free will can be maintained is to deny this fact and accept the credit or the blame for it. This is a trap that many people live in, and the confusion is entirely caused by the misunderstanding of who or what we are.

In his book *Brief Peeks Beyond*, philosopher Bernardo Kastrup defines free will in the following way:

'Free will is the capacity of an agent to make a choice unhindered by any factor outside that which the agent identifies itself with.'

The key aspect of this definition is what a person *'identifies themselves with'* rather than what a particular theory about reality defines or labels the person to be. It is ironic that materialism, the metaphysics that most people believe in, completely denies the possibility of free will. As far as materialism is concerned, your thoughts and feelings are determined by the physical, electrochemical processes in your brain.

Yet most people would reject the idea that the activities of neurons and synapses and the interactions among subatomic particles that make up a brain are an expression of their free will. We do not identify ourselves with brain function. You say 'I *have* a brain' rather than 'I *am* a brain'.

Indeed, how would you know you had a brain other than through second-hand sources of information? Before you started school, you developed and thrived without any knowledge or concept of what is between your ears or what it supposedly does.

Rather than experiencing brain function directly, what we experience is awareness of *thoughts, feelings, perceptions, and sensations*. This amalgam is what most people are referring to when they use the expression 'my mind.' And when they refer to 'me' or 'I'.

When you identify with *awareness* of experience, rather than with the physical structures of your brain and body and your thoughts and feelings, the problem of and confusion around the free will of 'you' as a separate individual disappears.

It Isn't About You

The intuition is that my will or choice is free *only* if it is solely determined by that which I perceive as 'me' or 'I'. We have already acknowledged the boundless, limitless nature of universal consciousness. So, recognition and acceptance of this awareness as *who I am*, by definition, entails free will.

Any thought, feeling, perception, or sensation can freely arise in awareness at any moment. This is the intuition of our freedom that we hold so dearly. And this includes the thought that arises a moment later, which claims, 'I thought that' or 'I chose that.' Or seems to decide, 'I like that' or 'I disapprove'.

But identification with the 'I' in those thoughts is optional.

The moment you let go of a particular idea of who you are – something that has a form, is responsible for thoughts, emotions, opinions, beliefs, preferences, a sense of purpose, who has or doesn't have free will – the problem of free will, like the hard problem of consciousness, becomes irrelevant.

Remember, this idea too, is a function of nature (the ground of which is awareness). It is something that awareness is doing. 'You' in this sense are being lived *by* nature. You are being thought *by* nature. You are being felt *by* nature. In fact, awareness is who or what *you* really are.

The whole thing isn't about a 'you', the idea who is the central character in the story of your life. That persona is something that nature (the real you) is enacting, or doing, just as golf is an activity that nature is doing through the activity of you. Identification with the form 'the golfer' is just a clumsy but functional artifact of a language that has evolved to describe duality.

The simple truth is; *'you' are that with which you identify.*

The Ultimate Meaning of Reality?

The realisation that your thinking isn't under control in the way most people believe it to be is troubling at first. But once the full implications are understood, the sense of freedom that ensues is well worth the short-term insecurity. A benefit is that you don't waste time and energy second-guessing your decisions. You accept the thinking that arose in that moment and the consequences and move on.

If the outcomes from a decision seem to be feelings of enjoyment and satisfaction, all well and good. If they don't, you learn from what happened. Again, notice that this isn't a conscious choice. It is the natural process that children follow before they start overthinking things and get in their own way.

This approach to life seems prevalent among the happiest, most successful people I encounter through my work across all sports.

Every day is a win-win feedback loop. Either progress is made, or learning occurs. Rinse and repeat. Failure isn't taken personally, and success doesn't seem to dull curiosity or the appetite to create and express themselves – or puff up the ego.

Regardless of the outcome, good or bad, there is a relentless desire to live a little bit more fully than yesterday. There is trust that through this process, at some point their full potential will be realised.

Human beings are a small aspect of reality. Therefore, their role in the ultimate meaning of nature or reality (if one exists) is likely a partial one. But alongside that argument is the fact that whatever human beings are, we are of the same essential nature as the whole. We are of the same source.

Therefore, the meaning of existence for human beings is unlikely to be completely disconnected from, or unrelated to, an underlying meaning of the universe. Nature is not static. It is a dynamic system. It seems to be doing something, going somewhere. There seem to be yet-unrealised potentials. The chance that we are completely unaligned or going in a different direction seems improbable.

Earlier, I presented evidence supporting the suggestion the purpose of life is to be happy. And that happiness is derived from knowing who you really are, your true self. When you put this idea alongside the recognition and acceptance that you are part of nature, not separate from it, an interesting possibility becomes apparent.

Nature seems to be evolving and developing using a similar model to the one favoured by happy human beings and communities. There may not be a pre-determined end goal. There is no supreme being in charge. The process is stochastic, instinctive. It involves experimentation, creating, trying things. Sometimes they work, and sometimes they don't.

Unfortunately (from a personal perspective) not every individual member of a species is happy or successful. Some fall by the wayside. But the collective learns and evolves from the mistakes and failures of the individual. This is a more nuanced and more interesting interpretation of Darwin's theory of evolution referenced earlier.

Metacognition is a comparatively recent upgrade in the psychology of human beings. We developed the capability for self-reflection and conscious self-awareness perhaps thirty thousand years ago. Clearly, we still have room for further evolution. It would be naïve to dismiss the idea that we might be in the middle of that process now.

Who knows what the human intellect might have access to and will be able to communicate after another thirty thousand years. Could the capacity for self-awareness and self-reflection be the evolutionary step that supercharges the way nature enhances awareness of itself?

The Implications of Idealism

If, as philosophical idealism describes, the ground of reality is mental rather than physical, how does this reconnect us with our ancestral traditions of the meaning of life as transcendence?

As stated in the previous chapter, human beings are driven by two primary motivations – feeling and understanding. Note these are aspects of mentality, not physical or biological drivers. If what is referred to as 'me' or 'I' is mental rather than physical in essence – a dissociated aspect of consciousness – then the end of your physical body is just the end of dissociation, *not* the end of consciousness or experience.

This hypothesis is supported with evidence from several different branches of neuroscience including those conducting research in psychedelics, pilots undergoing G-lock, near-death experiences, and cases of physical brain injury. In all these studies, a *decrease* in brain activity as measured in an fMRI brain scanner is accompanied by reported *expansion* in the richness and memorability of subjective experience.

Just as Aldous Huxley predicted in the 1950s, it would suggest that the death of the brain or body

CHAPTER 15: DID YOU CHOOSE TO PLAY GOLF?

leads to a liberation or expansion of experience, or consciousness. 'Personal' awareness is reintegrated with universal awareness. The transcendence of what is referred to as 'me' or 'I'.

The logical conclusion to this train of reasoning would be that when dissociation ends, all the insights, all the learning, all the felt experiences of your life are re-integrated into the universal consciousness. No experience is wasted, whether it is judged positive or negative, and no matter how small or seemingly insignificant.

When it comes to contemplating whether your life has meaning, there are profound implications on both personal and societal levels.

Every Shot Pleases Someone

As far as your golf is concerned, every snap hook, duffed chip, shanked bunker shot, yipped three-footer; every towering 3-iron, delicate pitch, and wise decision to lay up; every swing thought, great read on the putting green, and pure feeling of a nailed drive, all become part of the universal golfing mind.

Every shot you visualise, every anxious thought, every swing feeling, every brilliant tactical insight, all have meaning. Nothing you ever do on the golf course, or in any other aspect of your life is pointless or meaningless. It is all a part of the process of nature realising its potentials.

If you conclude that life or golf has no meaning, you have accepted all the faulty assumptions of materialism, and the assumption that all there is to know about ourselves and about reality is known. The latter is a pretty big call to make. A simpler, healthier, and more liveable position would be to admit we don't know.

To have doubts.

Even if you don't believe that what you are doing has any meaning, how do you know that? It's just a belief, and we know now how reliable belief is.

There is an equally valid alternative. That your golfing career, and your life in which the game holds a place, is sacred. Even if you are suffering now, the collective is learning and evolving. Every moment is an essential, fundamental experience in the mind of nature.

We know a lot less than we think we do. But this isn't a reason for insecurity or unhappiness. It is perfectly possible to live a contented, fulfilling life *not* having all the answers. Once you accept that you only know one thing for sure and the rest could be anything, a freedom and deep peace becomes available.

So, what do you know for sure? Where is the evidence for this alternative view?

Well, as confirmed in Part One, you know that

you are aware. You know that you are. There is something rather than nothing. And life is something nature is doing. You are not separate from nature. It's not about 'you' the individual. Nature is just doing what it does.

Human potential is about more than the personal. It starts with noticing our place in the bigger picture. As a species, we are a very recent occurrence.

We are tools of something unfathomably mysterious, greater and more powerful.

Playing with Freedom

So, at the risk of contradicting myself again, it seems to me, if there is a choice, it is a simple one. You can identify with something limited, finite, vulnerable, and capable of suffering. Or you can know yourself as the fundamental, essential, unlimited, infinite, deep-down whatever there is. And you can live your life and play your golf from either of those perspectives.

When you pull on your golf shoes and swing your bag onto your shoulder, you have assumed the part of 'the golfer', like an actor assuming a role in the play. You can fully immerse yourself in the character, experience the anticipation, the excitement, the agony, and the ecstasy that make the game both fascinating and addictive. And then when the final putt is sunk, you can take off the costume and flow back into the peace and freedom of your true nature.

Francis Lucille, one of my favourite teachers of the non-dual understanding, speaks about two types of freedom. *Freedom from* and *freedom to*. When you first see that escaping the limitations of identification with a limited, finite body and mind is possible, you begin to experience the *freedom from* – from fear, from insecurity, from anxiety, from meaninglessness.

As you live your life more from this understanding, you live from the peace, love, and happiness that comes from knowing your true nature. Instead of seeking happiness, or resisting unhappiness, you feel the *freedom to* – to create, to express your enthusiasm, to follow your passion, to play the game without worrying about the consequences, or whether what you or doing has, or needs to have any meaning.

You can deny reality by pretending it is something it isn't, and you can deny reality by refusing to engage with it. By walking away from the challenge. By refusing to play the game. But you are an aspect of nature. Trying to escape from it doesn't make sense.

You learn and live fully by engaging, by accepting what is.

When you step onto the first tee, whatever nature is doing, it is happening through you, playing the game.

Key Points from Chapter 15:

- You do not choose your thoughts. You cannot control what you think. You cannot choose to forget or not to think about something.
- When you say 'me' or 'I', you are referring to whatever you have become identified with.
- For most people, 'I' or 'me' means the body, the mind, and the ongoing story about them.
- You are not separate from nature. You are something that nature is doing.
- Your intuition that you have free will is a recognition of your true nature.

CHAPTER 16

Conclusion

'The privilege of a lifetime is to become who you truly are.'

Carl Gustav Jung

WELL, HERE WE ARE AT THE END OF THE BOOK. Thank you for sticking with it. I hope you have enjoyed the journey and can see the possibilities that arise from this new understanding about who you really are.

Pretty much every golfer I have met, regardless of their standard of play, spends far more time working on the physical side of the game than on learning about themselves, exploring the nature of their experience, or understanding why they play the game.

It's only when it seems that all the physical and technical avenues have been exhausted, when they are at the point of greatest frustration and disillusionment, that they turn and look in another direction.

This is what happened to me, leading to the exploration described in Part One.

When I came to understand how my experience of golf and life is created, when I accepted the primacy of the non-material aspects of the game, I found myself playing to my potential more often, learning faster with less effort and enjoying my golf more than ever. Many of my friends describe similar experiences.

In Part Two, we considered the implications for the mental side of golf. Confidence, creativity, concentration, consistency, and composure are concepts we are all familiar with. We are all aware that the feelings associated with them come and go. I have yet to meet a golfer who wouldn't like to know more about any of them, and to experience more of all of them.

If you are one of those golfers who came to this book in a time of struggle with your game, then I hope you can see potential for a different experience. In the coming weeks and months, just by being aware you will understand more about the nature of these feelings and where they come from.

Confidence is what you feel when you recognise the invulnerable, limitless, infinite reality of your true nature. When you know that you will be fine no matter what happens. When you understand that life happens in the present moment and that past and future only exist in memory and imagination.

CHAPTER 16: CONCLUSION

Confidence is accepting the ups and downs of the game – the excitement and the heartache – knowing that the numbers on your scorecard or someone else's opinions have nothing to do with and cannot affect who or what you are.

Creativity unfolds freely as you recognise the true source of all creation. Getting out of your own way is not a doing. It is a non-doing. It is the ceasing of an activity that makes you feel stuck or blocked. When you stop doing, when you stop trying to get somewhere or become something on behalf of your ego, that's when creativity begins to flow.

Life isn't about us as individuals. Life is a form of sacrificial service. A recognition that it's about serving something bigger than you. That you are a fundamental part of a greater whole. Creation is something that nature is doing as it realises its inherent potentials. The game of golf and the people that play it are small but essential elements of that universal creative process.

Consistency is found when you look inwards to recognise and play from the most consistent, permanent, infallible aspect of your experience. Most golfers look in the wrong direction. They seek consistency through perfecting the mechanics of the golf swing, or from attempting to control thought and feeling.

Mind and body are conditioned by experience.

Practice and preparation are part of the conditioning process but only useful if the patterns that develop are functional. If you practice from ignorance, of the ball flight laws or in misunderstanding who you really are, then the patterns are unlikely to be.

The purpose of preparation is to allow you to let go. Most golfers never trust enough to allow full expression of their potential.

Concentration is the experience of losing yourself in the present moment. Something grabs attention and curiosity draws you in. Interest, absorption, and fascination follow. This is flow or the zone. An experience of effortless engagement. A key characteristic of the zone is that you are no longer experienced as your individual self.

In a zone experience the 'I' thought is absent. Finding the zone becomes easier when you understand that awareness is what you are rather than something that you do. Telling yourself to focus or concentrate is a prime example of getting in your own way.

Composure is what you feel when you recognise the calm, peaceful, imperturbable, invulnerable essence of your true nature. This is who you really are. Awareness is untouched by experience. It is neither enhanced by a win nor diminished by failure. Its nature is unaffected by the experiences – good or bad – that are known by it.

This imperturbability is the essence of composure. Composure doesn't come from *what* you experience. It comes from the realisation that experience has no effect on who you really are. We don't play for the satisfaction of winning, or to avoid the disappointment of losing. Winning just allows seeking and resisting to end. When it does, you get out of the way and the feeling of connection to the source is revealed.

The golfer who understands this distinction will rarely lose composure.

What Is Mental Strength?

When these five characteristics are demonstrated, the impression is of what is referred to as mental strength. The label 'mentally strong' is usually situational. It is the outward appearance of a highly functional pattern of thinking in a particular, narrow set of circumstances.

Someone who seems mentally strong on the golf course might have less functional patterns of thinking in situations away from the game. For example, in their relationships with other people, with money, or with other objects or substances.

Patterns of thinking become conditioned by repetition in the same way that patterns of movement become conditioned through training and practice. As we have acknowledged, you can't control your thinking in the moment. But you can recognise and distinguish between a pattern of thinking that is helpful for a particular circumstance and one that isn't.

Your thinking is influenced by your beliefs and your values. Once an unhelpful pattern is identified, you can investigate the beliefs that give rise to and support it.

This then, is the process of getting out of your own way. It can be accomplished by taking small, incremental steps. It is a matter of learning which of your current beliefs gives rise to your thoughts and feelings in the moment. Of asking different questions. Of assembling the available evidence, then investigating that evidence using logic and reason.

You have probably taken the first step, in recognising that there is a voice in your head that pretends to be you and provides a running commentary on your golf game and other aspects of your life. Once you have noticed the voice, the next step is to investigate the belief that the voice is 'you'. Are you the thinker of troubling patterns of thought? Or are you what is aware of the voice, aware of the thoughts?

Once the truth is recognised, you can investigate the nature of that awareness. Again, use your experience rather than relying on beliefs. Is awareness something you are 'doing'? Is awareness still there when you stop 'doing' it? Does it come and go?

Does awareness have an edge, a boundary? This is crucial. Sometimes the absence of evidence can tell us as much as its presence. What are the implications of acknowledging the lack of evidence that your essential nature is bound by space and time?

Finally, what are the implications of knowing who you really are when the question *What does this mean to me?* arises, either on the golf course or anywhere else. Another way of encouraging this enquiry is to ask, *To whom does this matter?*

A thorough investigation can free you from much of the fear and anxiety that comes from attachment and identification with the body and the mind.

More Than One Reality?

Once it is established that awareness is not dependent upon anything, not bounded or limited, can there be a reality outside of awareness? If not, then consciousness must be the only reality – the reality that perceives. We are conditioned by our culture to believe that consciousness is some sort of 'mind created stuff.' Yet the evidence points to the opposite. The mind is known by awareness.

Our experience has two aspects – that which is perceived and that which perceives. That which is perceived, sometimes referred to as *mind*, is limited. I cannot know another person's thoughts. Minds are separate from one another. But we have already established that what knows the mind has no limits. Therefore, the awareness that knows my mind, and the awareness that knows your mind must be the same awareness.

Mind is limited. Awareness is not.

It is hard to dismiss the deep intuition that there is only one reality. Most physicists would concur with this conclusion. Many have spent their lives enhancing our perception and understanding of whatever this reality is. Yet that which can be perceived can only be as real as that which perceives it. And that which is perceived could be an illusion. But that which perceives cannot be.

The answer to *Am I aware?* can only be yes. If there is only one reality, then that which perceives must be that reality.

The word we use for 'that which perceives' is *awareness*, or *consciousness*.

An era defined by the story of separation between mind and body, between the spiritual and the material, is coming to an end. Whether you trust your inner wisdom pointing to a deep spiritual truth, or the evidence from multiple experiments in foundations of physics, the belief that 'you' are something limited, something finite, something that has a beginning and an end, is untenable. As we have discussed, the consequences of continuing to believe this are troubling, both on the golf course, and away from it.

What Do You Know for Sure?

The most detrimental aspect of the current narrative about the nature of reality is the belief that we know what it is and that it has no meaning beyond itself. Science and technology have been so successful that some scientists and many commentators on scientific matters promote the idea that we pretty much understand everything there is to be understood.

Yet a look back at the history of science proves that this is extremely naïve. As described at length by Thomas S Kuhn, we have been wrong about many things for a very long time. The Newtonian description of reality was revised by the work of Einstein. The description by Einstein was rendered incomplete by the work of Niels Bohr, Werner Heisenberg, and Erwin Schrodinger. At some point, the still mysterious world of quantum mechanics will be accurately described and then replaced with a new model.

When viewed in the light of the definition of meaning suggested earlier, the relational interpretation of quantum mechanics proposed by physicist Carlo Rovelli is a tantalising glimpse of a possible new direction for exploration.

The development of technology is heralded as evidence of our knowledge. But this is a convenient fiction. For technology to work, we just need an explanation of reality that works *as though it were* true. This doesn't mean that it *is* true. Einstein's model of reality and quantum mechanics disagree with each other. They cannot both be correct. Yet technologies developed using the models are very successful. Both theories work.

But that doesn't mean that we know what is really going on in terms of the true meaning or nature of reality.

This belief in the material model, the assumption that our understanding of the material world is complete and devoid of mystery robs our existence of meaning.

If we entertain the possibility that matter or physicality is simply what universal consciousness, the mind of nature (or god if you prefer) looks like from across the dissociative boundary of our personal mind, then several exciting possibilities open up for the way we feel, for the way we live our lives, and for how we approach the games we play.

The belief that reality is material, or physical, and can be fully described by a catalogue of numbers and equations leads inevitably to a bleak assumption, the soul destroying belief that all the insights you have collected during a lifetime, often due to significant trauma and suffering, are irrelevant.

All the achievements and attainments you strug-

CHAPTER 16: CONCLUSION

gled for, all the triumphs and disappointments and the lessons learned will someday all be forgotten as the planet we live on either burns up or dissolves back into the entropic soup from which it emerged.

Reconnecting with what our ancestors knew for thousands of years about the nature of reality and the true meaning of existence, that it is about *qualities of experience*, about feelings and understanding, not quantities, re-establishes the significance of every human life and experience.

Get Out of The Way of Nature

Your ego, the conceptualisation of who we are is another functional tool, but it isn't the truth. You need to know which mouth to put food in. But then to assert that who you really are is this limited, finite entity is to stretch the concept beyond its utility.

It is an assumption that leads to all the problems we have described earlier in terms of our biological early warning systems. Fear of short putts or the chipping yips are the result of a misunderstanding, not a character flaw.

Understanding what life is really about is an intuition, a feeling that comes from deep in our psyche. It is not something that can be known by thinking about it and making a logical, rational argument for it. Logic and reason are tools that can be used to disarm your ego and your intellect for long enough to allow you to feel, to trust. But knowing is not the result of a conceptualisation. It is before concepts.

It is something you embody, not believe.

Getting out of the way means allowing reality to do what it does through you. It was second nature to our ancestors. But our obsession with the personal, and celebration of the individual, got in the way. If nature is mental, then it's essential will is learning about meaning. That's what we are. We are meaning-making machines. Biology is an integral tool by which nature continuously unfolds and evolves. Metacognition is a very recent evolution of this biology.

Whatever it is that thinks and feels is not 'you', as in the body and the mind. The mind and body are experienced. They are not what experiences. Your personal self is known by your subjectivity, by awareness. This personal self -'You' is a thought. It is a feeling.

This is why the *Why?* question is a curse as well as a blessing. It is the mind searching for closure, for certainty. The quest to know why prevents us from stepping out of the way and just letting nature do what it does through us.

Your ego is also a tool of nature. It is the aspect of your mentality that is there to keep you alive. But nature doesn't care about your comfort or psychological safety. It doesn't give a damn whether you will look good in the eyes of your peers or whether you will get the credit for your achievements or the blame for your mistakes.

If you persist with the belief that life (and golf) is about you, as in your individual self, it will always be a struggle. You can't even imagine how to get out of your own way because you don't know who you are.

So, next time you head to the first tee, instead of playing the game of outcomes, of score, of achievement, try a different game.

Play the game of awareness. Awareness of the voice that is telling you what to do and how to do it. Awareness of the voice that points you to memories or to worries about the future. The voice that is concerned about results or what other people think.

Let it have its say, then just be aware of being aware.

Get out of the way and let nature play its game through you.

Bibliography

The Inner Game of Golf. W. Timothy Gallwey.

The Conscious Mind: In Search of a Fundamental Theory. David Chalmers.

The Structure of Scientific Revolutions. Thomas S Kuhn.

The World as Will and Representation: Volumes 1 & 2. Arthur Schopenhauer

Helgoland: The Strange and Beautiful Story of Quantum Physics. Carlo Rovelli

Rationalist Spirituality: An Exploration of Life and Existence Informed by Logic and Reason. Bernardo Kastrup

Brief Peeks Beyond: Critical essays on metaphysics, neuroscience, free will, skepticism and culture. Bernardo Kastrup

More than Allegory: On Religious Myth, Truth and Belief. Bernardo Kastrup

Why Materialism is Baloney: How True Skeptics Know There is no Death, and Fathom Answers to Life, the Universe and Everything. Bernardo Kastrup

You Are the Happiness You Seek: Uncovering the Awareness of Being. Rupert Spira

Being Aware of Being Aware: The Essence of Meditation. Volume 1. Rupert Spira

Man's Search for Meaning: The classic tribute to hope from the Holocaust. Victor E. Frankel

Skin in the Game: Hidden Assymetries in Daily Life. Nassim Nicholas Taleb.

Antifragile: Things That Benefit From Disorder. Nassim Nicholas Taleb

Dear Reader,

Just a short note to say thank you for buying and reading my book. I hope you enjoyed it and found some ideas that might help your game.

As mentioned in the text, I have two other books available. The first is *The Three Principles of Outstanding Golf*.

The second is *Take Relief*.

If you'd like to get in touch to have chat about your golf, or if you'd like to learn more about the ideas you have read in the book, please drop me an email to sam@samjarmangolf.com.

I offer one to one coaching on the mental side of the game either in person or online. You can find out more here samjarmangolf.com/discovery-call.

You can find my website at samjarmangolf.com. I'm on Twitter @samjarmangolf, or on Facebook at facebook.com/samjarmangolf.

Thanks again for reading, and all the best with your golf.

Kind regards,
Sam

About the author

Sam Jarman is a professional golfer, coach, author and speaker.

He played full time tournament golf for ten years, before realising that preventing other golfers making the same mistakes he was making could be more enjoyable and more lucrative than continuing to make them himself.

His first two books *The Three Principles of Outstanding Golf*, and *Take Relief* are fifty thousand word summaries of the most important thing he has learned; keep it simple.

"I finally saw the reason I was struggling to be the golfer I wanted to be. I also saw that the misunderstanding which prevents golfers from performing to their potential, is also responsible for the stress, worry, anxiety, boredom and lack of fulfilment which many people endure in their day to day lives.

I much prefer it when the people I know and like are enjoying what they do, so when I'm not playing tournaments, I help golfers, coaches and other athletes play better, learn better, work better and live better.

When we see our true nature, it frees us to be more inspired and productive, to enjoy life and work rather than endure them, and to be ourselves more often."

Sam lives in the Highlands of Scotland with Daisy, a charming but unreliable cocker spaniel. When he isn't teaching, writing about or playing golf he spends his time salmon fishing, skiing, reading, and enjoying the occasional pint of Guinness.

Printed in Great Britain
by Amazon